ESSENTIAL LIFE SKILLS SERIES

WHAT YOU NEED TO KNOW ABOUT

READING LABELS, DIRECTIONS & NEWSPAPERS

Second Edition

Carolyn Morton Starkey   Norgina Wright Penn

National Textbook Company
NTC a division of *NTC Publishing Group* • Lincolnwood, Illinois USA

ACKNOWLEDGMENTS

Beckley Post-Herald, Beckley Newspaper Corp., "Interstate Tunnel
    Detours Important"
Bristol-Myers Co., Arthritis Strength Bufferin Label
Campbell Soup Co., Home Style Beans label
Chicago Tribune, "Girls Don't Lag in Math, Study Finds," copyright
    ©1982, Chicago Tribune; "Pupils Go to Mat in Academic Olympics,"
    copyright © 1982, Chicago Tribune
General Foods Corp., JELL-O and Sugar Free JELL-O labels. JELL-O
    and Sugar Free JELL-O are registered trademarks of General Foods
    Corp.
The Kroger Co., Mixed Vegetables and Golden Corn labels
MURA Corp., MURA Hi-Stepper care instructions
Psychological Testing Corp., sample tests
Raleigh Register, Beckley Newspaper Corp., "The Roar of Motorcycles"
Richardson-Vicks, Inc., Vicks DayCare label

Preface

This revised edition from the Essential Life Skills Series tells you what you need to know about reading labels, newspapers, and directions. Mastering these reading skills will make you more assertive and self-confident. You will learn to cope better with everyday situations.

This book covers some familiar yet very important materials. You will learn to read and understand:

medicine labels	recipes
household product labels	test instructions
clothing labels	newspaper stories and editorials
food labels	newspaper indexes
step-by-step directions	classified ads

Throughout the book you will find examples of real labels, newspaper stories, and directions, like the ones you see and use every day.

Each section in this book includes definitions of words that may be new or difficult. Checkup sections help you review what you have learned. There are many opportunities to practice your skills.

Because of its flexible format, this book can be used either for self-study or in a group setting with an instructor. The answer key is on perforated pages so that it is easy to remove.

When you have mastered the skills in this book, you will want to develop other skills to become more successful in our modern world. The other books in the Essential Life Skills Series will show you how.

Essential Life Skills Series

What You Need to Know about Reading Labels, Directions & Newspapers 5655-2

What You Need to Know about Reading Ads, Reference Materials & Legal Documents 5656-0

What You Need to Know about Getting a Job and Filling Out Forms 5657-9

What You Need to Know about Reading Signs, Directories, Schedules, Maps, Charts & Utility Bills 5658-7

What You Need to Know about Basic Writing Skills, Letters & Consumer Complaints 5659-6

Contents

Reading labels

Do you ever read the labels on the products you buy? Government rules require manufacturers to include certain information on their labels. This information is put there to inform and protect you. As a consumer, you can make better buying decisions simply by reading a label.

A *food label* should tell you how much of a product a container holds. Perhaps you have noticed "Net Wt." (net weight) on a food label. A *medicine label* must warn you of the side effects of taking a medicine. For example, will a medicine make you dizzy or drowsy or weak? A *clothing label* should tell you how to care for a product. By reading a care label, you will learn whether to wash, bleach, or dry clean an item of clothing. *Household product labels* list various CAUTIONS and WARNINGS. Misuse of these products can be dangerous to your health.

The examples given above are examples of information *required* by law. In addition to this information, some manufacturers will tell you about a product's use and content. As a result, the amount you learn from a label will vary from product to product.

Medicine labels

WORDS TO KNOW

caution a warning

dose the amount of medicine to be taken at any one time

hazardous dangerous

over-the-counter medicine medicine you can buy without a doctor's prescription

pharmacist a person who is trained and licensed to dispense medicines

prescription a doctor's order for medicine

side effect an effect of a drug, such as an upset stomach, that is not the effect that was intended

symptom evidence of an illness, such as a fever or sore throat

Medicine labels contain the information you need to use medicines correctly. Medicines, of course, can be very helpful. They relieve symptoms and can reduce pain. They also stop aches. But remember that most medicines are drugs. They can be harmful, too. Therefore, it is very important to read medicine labels carefully. The label should be read *before* you use the medicine.

Labels on over-the-counter medicines

Over-the-counter medicines can be bought without a doctor's prescription. Labels on these medicines contain a great deal of information.

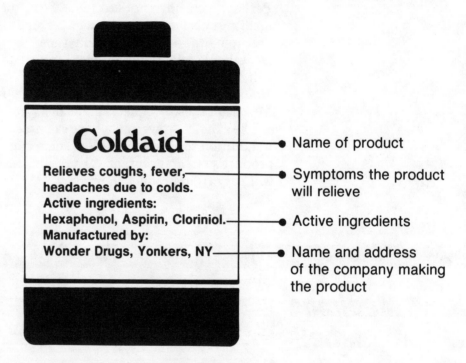

Coldaid ————————————● Name of product

Relieves coughs, fever, ————————● Symptoms the product
headaches due to colds. will relieve
Active ingredients:
Hexaphenol, Aspirin, Cloriniol. ————● Active ingredients
Manufactured by:
Wonder Drugs, Yonkers, NY ————————● Name and address
of the company making
the product

The label gives the name of the product: COLDAID. It also gives information about symptoms the medicine should relieve, its ingredients, and the manufacturer. You learn that COLDAID can be taken for colds, fevers, and headaches. You learn that it contains the drugs hex-a-phe-nol, clor-i-ni-ol, and aspirin. You learn that Wonder Drugs of Yonkers, New York, makes the product.

Over-the-counter medicine labels also give very specific directions for the use of a medicine.

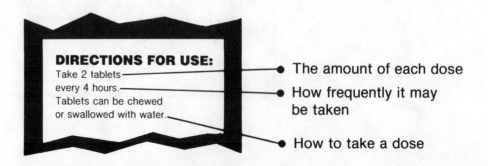

DIRECTIONS FOR USE:
Take 2 tablets ————————————● The amount of each dose
every 4 hours. ————————————● How frequently it may
Tablets can be chewed be taken
or swallowed with water. —————————● How to take a dose

The label will also give various warnings or cautions:

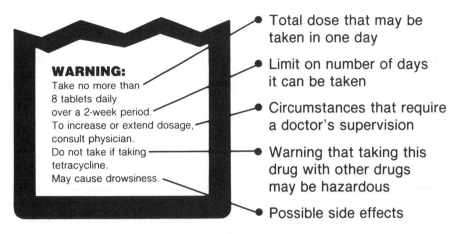

WARNING:
Take no more than
8 tablets daily
over a 2-week period.
To increase or extend dosage,
consult physician.
Do not take if taking
tetracycline.
May cause drowsiness.

• Total dose that may be taken in one day

• Limit on number of days it can be taken

• Circumstances that require a doctor's supervision

• Warning that taking this drug with other drugs may be hazardous

• Possible side effects

Activity 1

Interpreting labels on over-the-counter medicines

Study each of the following labels carefully. Answer the questions about each label.

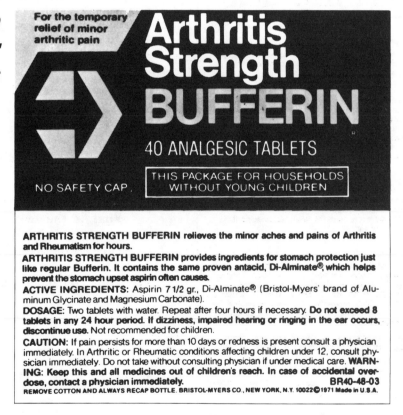

For the temporary relief of minor arthritic pain

Arthritis Strength BUFFERIN

40 ANALGESIC TABLETS

NO SAFETY CAP.

THIS PACKAGE FOR HOUSEHOLDS WITHOUT YOUNG CHILDREN

ARTHRITIS STRENGTH BUFFERIN relieves the minor aches and pains of Arthritis and Rheumatism for hours.

ARTHRITIS STRENGTH BUFFERIN provides ingredients for stomach protection just like regular Bufferin. It contains the same proven antacid, Di-Alminate®, which helps prevent the stomach upset aspirin often causes.

ACTIVE INGREDIENTS: Aspirin 7 1/2 gr., Di-Alminate®. (Bristol-Myers' brand of Aluminum Glycinate and Magnesium Carbonate).

DOSAGE: Two tablets with water. Repeat after four hours if necessary. Do not exceed 8 tablets in any 24 hour period. If dizziness, impaired hearing or ringing in the ear occurs, discontinue use. Not recommended for children.

CAUTION: If pain persists for more than 10 days or redness is present consult a physician immediately. In Arthritic or Rheumatic conditions affecting children under 12, consult physician immediately. Do not take without consulting physician if under medical care. WARNING: Keep this and all medicines out of children's reach. In case of accidental overdose, contact a physician immediately.   BR40-48-03
REMOVE COTTON AND ALWAYS RECAP BOTTLE. BRISTOL-MYERS CO., NEW YORK, N.Y. 10022©1971 Made in U.S.A.

1. What is the name of this product?_____

2. What symptoms is this product supposed to relieve?_____

3. How much of this product is to be taken for each dose? _____

4. How often should a dose be taken? _____

   What is the maximum number of tablets that can be taken in a 24-hour period? _____

5. What signals mean that you should see a doctor? _____

   _____

6. What other cautions should the buyer observe? _____

   _____

CONSUMER INFORMATION

Vicks DayCare
DAYTIME COLDS MEDICINE

PURPOSE OF PRODUCT:
To provide hours of relief from the nasal congestion, coughing, aches and pains, and cough irritated throat of a cold or flu without drowsy side effects.

BENEFITS FROM PRODUCT:
• helps clear stuffy nose, congested sinus openings
• calms, quiets coughing
• eases headache pain and the ache-all-over feeling
• soothes cough irritated throat
• No drowsy side effects. Non-narcotic
Relieves these cold symptoms to let you get your day off to a good start.

DIRECTIONS FOR USE:
ADULTS: 12 and over—one fluid ounce in medicine cup provided (2 tablespoonfuls)
CHILDREN: 6-12—one-half fluid ounce in medicine cup provided (1 tablespoonful)
May be repeated every four (4) hours as needed. Maximum 4 doses per day.

WARNING:
Do not administer to children under 6 years of age unless directed by physician. Persistent cough may indicate the presence of a serious condition. Persons with a high fever or persistent cough or with high blood pressure, diabetes, heart or thyroid disease should not use this preparation unless directed by physician. Do not use more than ten days unless directed by physician.

Do not exceed recommended dosage unless directed by physician. KEEP OUT OF REACH OF CHILDREN.

ACTIVE INGREDIENTS:
Each fluid ounce contains Acetaminophen 600 mg., Dextromethorphan Hydrobromide 20 mg., Phenylpropanolamine Hydrochloride 25 mg.   Alcohol 7.5%

1. What is the name of this product? _____

   _____

2. List the symptoms this product is supposed to relieve. _____

   _____

3. How much of this product is to be taken for each dose? _____

4. How often may a dose be taken? _____

   _____

   What is the maximum amount of this product that can be taken in a 24-hour period? _____

5. What signals mean that you should stop using this product? _____

   _____

6. What other cautions should the buyer observe?

   _____

4

Labels on prescription medicines

Only a doctor can order prescription drugs. Your doctor tells your pharmacist how you are to use a medicine. When the prescription is filled, the pharmacist types the doctor's instructions on the label. These instructions tell you how much medicine to take at one time. They also tell how often to take the medicine. Unlike over-the-counter labels, prescription labels may not tell what a medicine is for. They may not list side effects. They may not give special cautions. Sometimes even the name of the medicine is not on the label. You may have to ask your doctor for this additional information.

Remember, labels are on medicines for a reason. They tell you how to use a medicine correctly. The law requires that labels carry important information. But the information is useless unless you read and follow it.

Activity 2

Interpreting labels on prescription medicines

Complete the statements about each of the following prescription labels.

SAM'S DRUGS

14200 FENKELL AVE.   DETROIT, MICH.

PHONES VE 7-2838 and 7-1575

Reg. No. 8765   B No 2345

Patient Geri Purshing

Address 43 North

Take 2 twice daily.

Dr. Pillston   Reg. No. 2121

Address 34 South   Date 5/3

This Prescription cannot be refilled nor a copy given.

1. _____ is the only person who should take this medicine.

2. _____ pill(s) should be taken for each dose.

3. The person who prescribed this medicine is _____ .

4. A total of _____ pills should be taken in a day.

5. The patient can have this prescription refilled _____ times.

```
                    SAM'S DRUGS
              14200 FENKELL AVE.    DETROIT, MICH.
              PHONES VE 7-2838 and 7-1575
       Reg. No. 8765              R No.  2346
     Patient  Vicki Urkan
     Address  543 East

          Take 1 every 4 hours.

     Dr.  Jaons                 Reg. No.  2323
     Address 23 Bend            Date      4/5
        This Prescription cannot be refilled nor a copy given.
```

1. _____ is the only person who should take this medicine.

2. _____ pill(s) should be taken for each dose.

3. The person who prescribed this medicine is _____ .

4. A total of _____ pills should be taken in a day.

5. The patient can have this prescription refilled _____ times.

CHECK YOUR UNDERSTANDING OF MEDICINE LABELS

Here are some words to know when reading a medicine label. Use these words to find the correct word or words for the following sentences.

prescription	symptom	caution
side effect	dose	

1. The _____ from some medicines may be an upset stomach.

2. One _____ of a cold is a stuffy nose.

3. A label may _____ you not to take more than 4 pills in 24 hours.

4. The _____ of a medicine is the amount that can be taken at one time.

5. The doctor gave me a _____ for penicillin when I had a sore throat.

6

Household products labels

WORDS TO KNOW
dilute to make weaker or thinner by adding liquid, usually water
discoloration changed or spoiled color
puncture to make a small hole with a pointed object
ventilate to allow fresh air to enter
flammable easily set on fire

Always read the labels on household products. Many of these products, like medicines, can harm you. Air fresheners, insect sprays, detergents, and many other products you use every day must be used with care. Give close attention to the labels on these products. These labels give cautions and warnings. They tell you how to use a product safely. In case you have an accident with a product, the label will tell you exactly what to do.

Activity 3

Reading labels on household products

Read the following labels. Decide whether the statements about them are TRUE (T) or FALSE (F).

ROXO BLEACH

CAUTION: Roxo bleach may be harmful if swallowed or may cause severe eye irritation if splashed in eyes. If swallowed, give milk. If splashed in eyes, flood with water. Call physician. Skin irritant; if contact with skin, wash off with water. Do not use bleach with ammonia or products containing acids, such as toilet-bowl cleaners, rust removers, or vinegar. To do so will release hazardous gases. Prolonged contact with metal may cause pitting or discoloration. Do not use this bottle to store any liquid other than bleach.

_____ 1. This product is not harmful to the skin.

_____ 2. Used with ammonia, this product becomes harmless.

_____ 3. This product can cause severe eye irritation.

_____ 4. This product is harmful if swallowed.

_____ 5. The bottle may be safely used for storing other liquids.

FLYING INSECT KILLER

FLAMMABLE—Contents under pressure. Do not use near fire, spark, or flame. Never puncture or throw container into fire. Never set container on stove, radiator, or places where temperature may exceed 120º F., which may cause it to burst. Foods should be removed or covered during treatment. All food processing surfaces should be covered during treatment or thoroughly cleaned before using. When using the product in these areas, apply only when the facility is not in operation. Do not remain in treated areas. Ventilate the areas after treatment is completed. Keep out of reach of children. Remove pets and cover fish aquariums before spraying.

_____ **1.** It is not necessary to ventilate the room where this product is used.

_____ **2.** It is safe to remain in the area after using this product.

_____ **3.** Foods should be removed or covered when using this product.

_____ **4.** This product will not harm pets.

_____ **5.** This product should be stored in areas where the temperature is at least 120°F.

_____ **6.** It is all right to spray this product near a fire.

_____ **7.** The can will burst if it becomes very hot.

_____ **8.** Dishes should be covered when this product is used.

_____ **9.** The contents of the can are not under pressure.

_____ **10.** This product should be kept away from children.

Activity 4

Reading labels on household products

Read the following labels. Complete the statements about each product.

AMMONIA
FIRST AID

External: Flood with water, then wash with vinegar.

Internal: Give large quantities of diluted vinegar or juice of lemon, grapefruit, or orange. Call physician.

Eyes: Rinse thoroughly with water, preferably warm, for 15 minutes. Get prompt medical attention.

If this happens

1. Product in the eyes

2. Product accidentally swallowed

3. Product on hands

4. Product on arms

You should

1. _____

2. _____

3. _____

4. _____

RED DEMON LYE
FIRST AID

Skin: Flush with water for 15 minutes.

Eyes: Immediately hold face under running water for 20 minutes with eyes open, by force if necessary.

In mouth or if swallowed: Clear mouth. Do not induce vomiting. Give [drink] large quantities of water or milk. Give at least 2 ounces to maximum of one pint equal parts of vinegar and water, followed by olive oil or cooking oil (by teaspoon). **Transport victim to nearest medical facility or call physician immediately.**

If this happens

1. Product in the eyes

2. Product accidentally swallowed

3. Product on hands

4. Product on arms

You should

1. _____

2. _____

3. _____

4. _____

9

Read the following label and answer the questions about it.

Sheen Furniture Wax

SHEEN wax leaves a clean, tough shine and helps protect the natural beauty of your furniture against spills, stains, and ordinary wear.

DIRECTIONS: SHAKE WELL BEFORE USE!
Hold can upright about six inches from surface. For normal use, spray lightly. For more thorough cleaning, spray surface generously. Wipe immediately with a clean, dry cloth. For small items and hard-to-reach places, spray on cloth and polish.

CAUTION: Do not use near fire or flame. Do not set or store container where temperature exceeds 120 F. as container may burst. Do not puncture or incinerate. Do not spray or use on floors. Keep out of reach of children.

1. What should you do if you want to thoroughly clean a piece of furniture with this product?

_____

2. What might happen if this product is stored in a very warm place? _____

3. What must you do first before using this product? _____

4. Where should this product *not* be used? _____

5. What would happen if you threw the empty can into an apartment building incinerator?

_____

6. When using this product, how far away from the surface of furniture should you hold the can? _____

7. Is it OK to spray furniture with this product then wait for 30 minutes before wiping the furniture? _____

Clothing labels

WORDS TO KNOW

bleach   to make whiter or lighter in color

drip-dry   to dry without wrinkles when hung up dripping wet

dry-clean   to clean without water

hand wash   to wash something by hand

machine wash   to wash in a washing machine

permanent press   describes material specially treated to make it hold its shape and resist wrinkling when washed

The law says that clothing you buy must carry certain labels. Clothing tags and labels come in many shapes and sizes. These labels tell you what brand name you're buying. They tell you what various items of clothing are made of. And they tell you how to care for these items. Following the instructions on care labels helps you get the most wear and satisfaction from the clothes you buy. Labels that tell you how to care for an item of clothing must be *permanent*. They are usually woven or printed labels. They will be found inside clothing. They are often sewn into seams.

Activity 5

Reading clothing labels

Harriet Foster bought a very expensive dress made of special fabric. The label shown here came inside the dress. Are the statements about the care label TRUE (T) or FALSE (F)?

> DO NOT BLEACH. MACHINE WASH AND TUMBLE DRY AT PERMANENT-PRESS CYCLE. REMOVE FROM DRYER AS SOON AS CYCLE STOPS.

_____ **1.** Harriet can wash this dress, but only by hand.

_____ **2.** Harriet cannot use bleach when washing this dress.

_____ **3.** Harriet's dress must be dried on a clothesline.

_____ **4.** Harriet's dress can go in her dryer, but she must use a permanent-press cycle.

_____ **5.** For the best results, Harriet should remove her dress from the dryer as soon as the dryer stops.

Activity 6

Reading clothing labels

Read the instructions on the labels below. Answer the questions about the labels. Use the letter with each label to answer the questions.

A

DO NOT DRY-CLEAN

HAND WASH ONLY
– DRIP DRY

IRON ON
REVERSE SIDE
WITH COOL IRON

B

DRY-CLEAN

TOUCH-UP WITH
WARM IRON

C

MACHINE WASH
AND DRY

STEAM IRON AT
MEDIUM SETTING

D

HAND WASH–
LINE-DRY

STEAM IRON AT
WARM SETTING

E

MACHINE WASH
AT COLD SETTING
– GENTLE CYCLE

DRIP-DRY

IRON ON
REVERSE SIDE
WITH COOL IRON

F

MACHINE WASH
AND DRY AT
WARM SETTINGS

IRON WHILE
DAMP WITH
WARM IRON

G

MACHINE WASH
WARM

LINE-DRY ONLY

IRON ON
REVERSE SIDE
WITH COOL IRON

H

HAND WASH–
DRIP-DRY

STEAM IRON AT
WARM SETTING

1. Which item of clothing must be dry-cleaned? _____

2. Which items should be hand washed only? _____

3. Which items require steam ironing? _____

4. Which item must not be dry-cleaned? _____

5. Which items must not be dried in a dryer? _____

6. Which items should be machine washed in warm water? _____

7. Which items should be ironed on the wrong side? _____

8. Which item should be ironed while damp? _____

CHECK YOUR UNDERSTANDING OF CLOTHING LABELS

Read the following label. Then answer the questions about it.

> Permanent Press 60% Polyester 40% Cotton
> Machine wash in warm water with like colors.
> No bleach. Tumble dry at medium setting.

1. The words "permanent press" on a garment mean _____

_____ .

2. To wash with "like colors" means to _____

_____ .

3. Can this garment be bleached? _____

4. Can this garment be dried in a clothes dryer? _____

5. Should this garment be washed in hot water? _____

Food labels

WORDS TO KNOW

calories   the energy value in a food

carbohydrate   a class of foods, including sugars and starches, that provide nourishment and promote growth

ingredients   the contents of a particular product

minerals   nonliving substances that can either occur in nature or be man made. Some minerals, such as salt, are used for seasoning food.

nutrients   food substances that sustain life and promote growth

protein   an organic substance needed for cell growth. Meat, eggs, and fish are rich in protein.

serving size   the amount of food usually eaten by one person as part of a meal. Nutrition information is usually given on the basis of one serving.

You will find a lot of information on the labels of the foods you buy. Food labels should give you at least *three* important pieces of information.

▶ the name of a product (BRAND NAME)
▶ how much of a product you're getting (NET WEIGHT)
▶ who makes the product (NAME AND ADDRESS OF THE MANUFACTURER OR DISTRIBUTOR)

Many labels list ingredients and give nutrition information. Ingredients are listed in order of their amounts in the product, beginning with the most plentiful ingredient. Nutrition information is usually found on the back of a label. If you read this information, you will find the number of calories and the grams of protein, carbohydrate, and fat in a single serving. The serving size is also given. Food labels also list certain vitamins and minerals. These nutrients are listed with the percent one serving provides of a person's daily needs.

brand name

nutrition information

vitamins & minerals in one serving

ingredients in order by amount

manufacturer's name and address

net weight

Activity 7
Reading food labels

Read the nutrition information on the following labels. Answer the questions below each label.

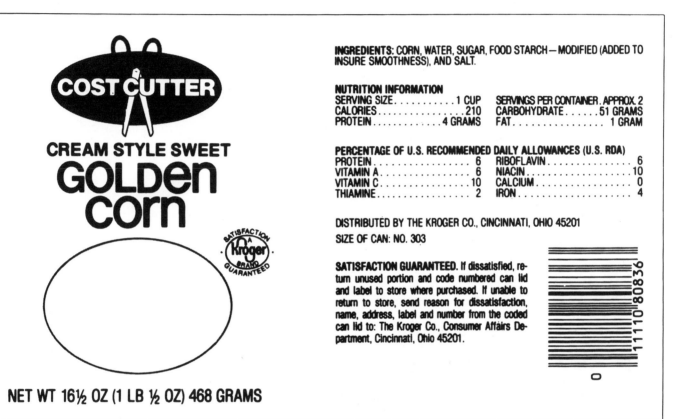

COST CUTTER

CREAM STYLE SWEET
GOLDen corn

Kroger SATISFACTION GUARANTEED A BRAND

NET WT 16½ OZ (1 LB ½ OZ) 468 GRAMS

INGREDIENTS: CORN, WATER, SUGAR, FOOD STARCH—MODIFIED (ADDED TO INSURE SMOOTHNESS), AND SALT.

NUTRITION INFORMATION
SERVING SIZE. . . . . 1 CUP   SERVINGS PER CONTAINER. APPROX. 2
CALORIES. 210   CARBOHYDRATE. . . . . . 51 GRAMS
PROTEIN. . . . . 4 GRAMS   FAT. . . . . 1 GRAM

PERCENTAGE OF U.S. RECOMMENDED DAILY ALLOWANCES (U.S. RDA)
PROTEIN. 6   RIBOFLAVIN. 6
VITAMIN A. 6   NIACIN. 10
VITAMIN C. 10   CALCIUM. 0
THIAMINE. 2   IRON. 4

DISTRIBUTED BY THE KROGER CO., CINCINNATI, OHIO 45201

SIZE OF CAN: NO. 303

SATISFACTION GUARANTEED. If dissatisfied, return unused portion and code numbered can lid and label to store where purchased. If unable to return to store, send reason for dissatisfaction, name, address, label and number from the coded can lid to: The Kroger Co., Consumer Affairs Department, Cincinnati, Ohio 45201.

1. One serving of Cost Cutter Corn is equal to _____ .

2. One can of corn gives you _____ one-cup servings.

3. There are _____ calories in a serving.

4. Cost Cutter Corn has vitamin _____ and vitamin _____ .

5. A serving of corn will give you _____ percent of the amount of protein you need daily.

6. There is 0% _____ in Cost Cutter Corn.

Kroger

MIXED
VEGETABLES

241
GRAMS

NET WT
8½ OZ

INGREDIENTS: CARROTS, POTATOES, CELERY, SWEET PEAS, GREEN BEANS, CORN, LIMA BEANS, WATER, SALT AND GROUND ONION.

NUTRITION INFORMATION PER SERVING

SERVING SIZE: 1 CUP SERVINGS PER CONTAINER: APPROX. 1
CALORIES .... 70 CARBOHYDRATE .... 14 g
PROTEIN .... 2 g FAT .... 0 g

PERCENTAGE OF RECOMMENDED DAILY ALLOWANCES (U.S. RDA)
PROTEIN 4
VITAMIN A 250
VITAMIN C 10
THIAMINE 2
RIBOFLAVIN 6
NIACIN 4
CALCIUM 4
IRON 8
DISTRIBUTED BY THE KROGER CO., CINCINNATI, OHIO 45201

· UNCONDITIONALLY GUARANTEED ·
Kroger's First Quality

1. One serving of mixed vegetables is equal to _____ .

2. This can contains _____ serving(s).

3. There are only _____ calories in a serving.

4. There are _____ grams of protein and _____ grams of carbohydrate in a serving.

5. There is no _____ in this food.

6. This food contains vitamins _____ and _____ .

7. The protein in a serving of mixed vegetables is only _____ percent of the total amount of protein you need daily.

8. List the ingredients in this product. _____

_____

9. What is the net weight of this product? _____

10. One serving of mixed vegetables will give you _____ percent of the iron you need daily according to the U.S. RDA.

Activity 8

Reading and comparing food labels

Read and compare the nutrition information on the following labels. Answer the questions about these labels.

JELL-O Gelatin Dessert

NUTRITION INFORMATION • SERVING SIZE: 1/2 CUP • SERVINGS PER PACKAGE: 4
CALORIES......60 PROTEIN........2 g — NOT A SIGNIFICANT SOURCE OF PROTEIN
CARBOHYDRATE......19 g FAT......0 SODIUM......50 mg
CONTAINS LESS THAN 2% OF THE U.S. RECOMMENDED DAILY ALLOWANCES (U.S. RDA)
OF VITAMIN A, VITAMIN C, THIAMINE, RIBOFLAVIN, NIACIN, CALCIUM AND IRON.
INGREDIENTS: SUGAR, GELATIN, ADIPIC ACID (FOR TARTNESS), DISODIUM PHOS-
PHATE (CONTROLS ACIDITY), FUMARIC ACID (FOR TARTNESS), ARTIFICIAL
COLOR, ARTIFICIAL FLAVOR.   85 g
GENERAL FOODS CORPORATION, WHITE PLAINS, NY 10625, U.S.A.

Sugar Free JELL-O Gelatin Dessert

NUTRITION INFORMATION PER SERVING • SERVING SIZE: 1/2 CUP • SERVINGS PER PACKAGE: 4
CALORIES... 8 PROTEIN... 1g CARBOHYDRATE...0 FAT...0 SODIUM...50mg
NOT A SIGNIFICANT SOURCE OF PROTEIN. CONTAINS LESS THAN 2% OF THE U.S.
RECOMMENDED DAILY ALLOWANCES (U.S. RDA) OF VITAMIN A, VITAMIN C, THIA-
MINE, RIBOFLAVIN, NIACIN, CALCIUM AND IRON.
INGREDIENTS: GELATIN, ADIPIC ACID (FOR TARTNESS), MALTODEXTRIN (FROM
CORN), DISODIUM PHOSPHATE (CONTROLS ACIDITY), ASPARTAME** (SWEETENER),
FUMARIC ACID (FOR TARTNESS), ARTIFICIAL COLOR, SALT, ARTIFICIAL FLAVOR.
8.5g   GENERAL FOODS CORP.,
**PHENYLKETONURICS: CONTAINS PHENYLALANINE   WHITE PLAINS, NY 10625, U.S.A.

1. How many calories are in one serving of Sugar Free Jell-O? _____

2. How many calories are in one serving of regular Jell-O? _____

3. How many carbohydrates are in a serving of regular Jell-O? _____

4. What kind of sweetener is used in Sugar Free Jell-O? _____

5. Are these products significant sources of protein? _____

6. List the ingredients found in each of these products.

Sugar Free Jell-O

_____

_____

_____

_____

_____

Regular Jell-O

_____

_____

_____

_____

_____

7. Give the name and address of the manufacturer of these two products. _____

_____

CHECK YOUR UNDERSTANDING OF FOOD LABELS

Read the following food label and answer the questions about it.

Nutrition Information Per Portion

Portion size . . 6 oz.	Portions per container . 2
calories 40	carbohydrate . . . . 9 grams
protein . . . . . 1 gram	fat . . . . 0 grams

Percentages of U.S. Recommended Daily Allowances (U.S. RDA)

protein 2%	niacin 8%
vitamin A . . . 25%	calcium . . . . *
vitamin C . . . 15%	iron 6%
thiamin 4%	phosphorus 4%
riboflavin . . . 2%	magnesium 4%

*Contains less than 2% of the U.S. RDA of this nutrient.

Ingredients: tomatoes, salt, dehydrated onions, dehydrated garlic, and natural flavors.

1. There are _____ calories in one portion.

2. The main ingredient in this product is _____ .

3. This container holds _____ portions.

4. The protein in a serving of this product is _____% of the total amount of protein you need daily.

5. This product is fairly high in vitamin _____ .

Following directions

Following directions requires special reading skills. Some directions are general; others are very specific. You must read specific directions *completely* to get the whole picture. *All* information must be read very carefully. If you don't read and follow directions, an item may not operate properly. You may spoil something you are cooking. You may fail a test simply because you did not mark an answer card correctly.

In this section, you will practice reading both general and specific directions. They will be the kind of directions you see most often. For example, you will learn how to fold a letter and set a digital watch. You will also practice reading recipes. Recipes are only one example of the step-by-step directions you will study in this chapter. Finally, you will study different kinds of tests and practice following test directions.

Reading directions

WORDS TO KNOW

abrasive   something rough used to smooth or polish

assemble   to fit parts together

detergent   a soap substitute used for washing and cleaning

immerse   to lower (something) into liquid until it is completely covered

peak performance   the best possible performance

sequence   a regular order, as by number or date

Most directions tell you how to assemble or use something. You may have followed such directions if you've ever put together a kite or folded a box. Often directions tell you to follow a certain order. You must read and understand what should be done first, second, and so on, until the job is done.

Some directions stress DO and DON'T, especially DON'T. If you don't pay attention to these warnings, you could ruin a new watch or vacuum cleaner or TV set.

Activity 1

Reading directions

The directions that follow tell you how to clean a blender. Read the questions that follow the directions. Select the phrase that correctly completes each statement about the blender.

HOW TO CLEAN YOUR BLENDER

Your new blender has been designed to give you years of enjoyment, with a minimum amount of care.

To make sure that your blender always operates at peak performance, you should clean the container after each and every use. Please do not use the container to store foods or beverages.

We recommend that you treat your blender container with the same care that you give to your good glassware.

If you have been blending solid foods, you may want to clean the container first with a long-handled brush and warm water to dislodge any food particles that cling to the inside.

After blending ANYTHING—liquid or solid—you should ALWAYS follow this procedure:

1. Put about one cup of warm water and a dash of detergent into your blender container, cover and blend, at a low speed, for about 30 seconds.

2. Rinse and dry the container. (Here's a quick tip: To make sure it is really dry, put it back on your blender base, cover and run the blender, empty, at a low speed, for about 2 to 5 seconds, so that any remaining water drops may evaporate.)

3. To clean your blender base, unplug and use a soft cloth or sponge, warm water and a mild detergent. Do not immerse blender in water, and do not use any harsh or abrasive cleansers.

_____ **1.** To make sure your blender operates at peak performance, clean the container
    a. every time you use it.
    b. as little as possible.
    c. as often as possible.

_____ **2.** You should not use the container to
    a. store foods.
    b. store beverages.
    c. store foods or beverages.

_____ **3.** After blending solid foods,
    a. clean the container with a brush and warm water.
    b. clean the container with a brush and cold water.
    c. clean the container with cold water.

_____ **4.** The base of this blender
   a. cannot be placed in water.
   b. cannot take harsh cleaners.
   c. cannot be placed in water and cannot take harsh or abrasive cleaners.

These are the steps involved in cleaning the blender:
1) Rinse and dry the blender container.
2) Put a cup of warm water with detergent into the blender.
3) Put the blender on its base and run the blender at a low speed for 2 to 5 seconds.
4) Unplug the blender base and clean it with a soft cloth, warm water, and detergent.
5) Blend detergent and water at a low speed for about thirty seconds.

_____ **5.** The correct order of these steps is
   a. 4, 2, 5, 3, 1.
   b. 2, 5, 1, 4, 3.
   c. 2, 5, 4, 3, 1.

Activity 2

Following step-by-step directions

Do you know the correct way to fold a business letter? Which way do you place the letter in the envelope? What do you do when your envelope is too short? Below are the steps for folding a business letter to fit (1) a standard-size business envelope (about 9½ × 4⅛ inches in size) and (2) a short envelope (about 3½ × 6½ inches in size).

1. Folding a Business Letter for a Standard-Size Envelope

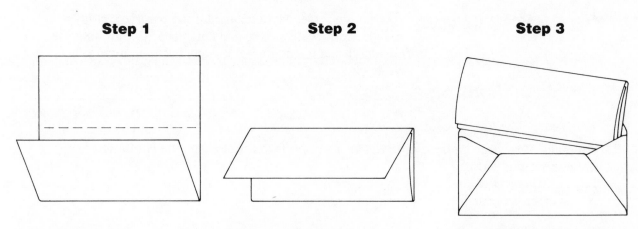

Step 1

Fold bottom up one-third.

Step 2

Fold top down, leaving about one-quarter inch of the paper showing below the edge.

Step 3

Place letter in envelope with open flap facing you, ready to be unfolded.

2. Folding a Business Letter for a Short Envelope

Step 1	**Step 2**	**Step 3**	**Step 4**
	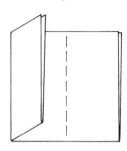	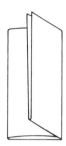	
Fold paper in half, bottom side up.	Fold in thirds, left side first . . .	. . . then right side, leaving about one-quarter inch of the paper showing past the edge.	Place letter in envelope with open flap facing you.

In this activity you will need a standard-size business envelope, a short envelope, and a sheet of either typing paper or looseleaf notebook paper. Using the steps shown above,
a. fold a letter and correctly place in a business envelope.
b. fold a letter and correctly place in a short envelope.

Activity 3
Following directions

Have you ever bought a radio, cassette player, or record player? If you have, you know that these items come with a set of instructions for the proper use and care of the equipment. Read the following owner's manual. It is for the type of radio that clips to your belt and has a lightweight headset.

After reading the owner's manual, decide whether the following statements about the instructions for the radio and headset are TRUE (T) or FALSE (F).

MURA
hi stepper™

Your new 'hi stepper' portable headphone radio has been designed to provide you with high fidelity FM stereo listening as well as excellent FM monoral reception.

In order to obtain the fullest enjoyment from your 'hi stepper' we suggest that you read the operating instructions carefully before using your new radio.

23

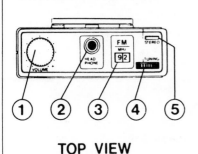

1. Volume Control
2. Headphone Socket/
   Automatic Shut-Off
3. Dial Window
4. Tuning Control
5. FM Stereo Indicator
6. Built-in Clip
7. Balance Control
8. ON/OFF/BAND
   Selector Switch
9. Battery Compartment

TOP VIEW

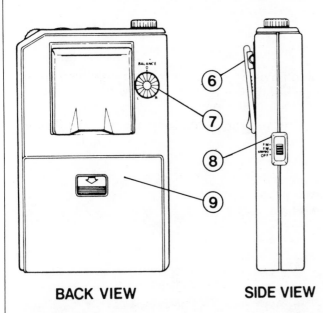

BACK VIEW   **SIDE VIEW**

Operation:

1) First insert 4 fresh penlite batteries (size AA or UM3) in the battery compartment (9). Care should be taken to ensure the batteries are inserted in the correct polarity positions as shown on the diagram in the battery compartment.

2) Fully uncoil the headphone cord and insert the headphone plug into the headphone socket (2). Place the headphones on your head while observing that the ear piece with the 'L' mark should be placed over the left ear and the ear piece with the 'R' mark over the right ear. Adjust the head band so that the ear pieces fall comfortably over the center of each ear.

3) Use the ON/OFF/BAND Selector Switch (8) to switch the set on to the FM position. Adjust the Volume Control (1) to a comfortable listening level.

4) Next use the Tuning Control (4) to select your station. The station frequency can be seen in the dial window.

5) If you wish to listen to FM stereo broadcasts, the Band Switch (8) must be in the FM Stereo position. When tuning the radio in this position the Stereo Indicator (5) will light whenever you tune in a station which is broadcasting in stereo. If the stereo indicator flickers and does not stay lighted this indicates that the station you are receiving is too weak and good stereo reception is not possible. If you still wish to listen to this station you must switch from FM Stereo to FM. This will eliminate the hissing and distortion of the weak stereo signal and allow you to listen to this station in monoral FM.

6) After selecting your station and adjusting the volume level it may be necessary to adjust the Balance Control (7) located on the rear of the set. This control will balance the volume level between the left and right headphone receiver so that equal volume is heard in each ear. Once adjusted it should not be necessary to re-adjust this control unless another person is using your set.

7) The built-in Clip (6) at the rear of the set may be used for securing the set to your belt or clipping it in your pocket.

Recommendations:

HEADPHONES—Inasmuch as the lead wire from the headphones to the set acts as your FM antenna, this wire should always be fully extended. If for safety or comfort reasons it is necessary to bunch up or secure excess wire this should be done on the end nearest the headphones and not near the set.

AUTOMATIC SHUT-OFF—Since your set does not have a loudspeaker to remind you that it is turned on, a specially designed headphone socket has been provided as an alternate means to shut off all power to your set. Even though the switch (8) remains in one of the "ON" positions, all power will shut off whenever the headphone plug is removed from the headphone socket.

BATTERIES—In order to protect your set and obtain maximum battery life we recommend that you use high quality batteries. Additional battery life may be obtained by using alkaline batteries. Since no batteries are completely leak proof we recommend that you remove the batteries from your set during long periods of infrequent use.

CARE AND CLEANING—The cabinet of your set may be cleaned with a damp soft cloth but no solvents or abrasives should be used. Should the ear pads on your headphones become soiled, these may be removed from the headphones, washed in mild soap and water and allowed to air dry.

SERVICE—Should your set become dead, weak, distorted, fail to receive stereo signals, or act improperly in any manner it is most commonly caused by weak batteries. Before returning your set for servicing always test it first with a new set of fresh batteries.

SAFETY PRECAUTIONS

YOUR NEW 'HI STEPPER' PROVIDES YOU WITH PRIVATE RADIO RECEPTION BUT AT THE SAME TIME IT MAY PREVENT YOU FROM HEARING OUTSIDE SOUNDS WHILE YOU ARE WEARING THE HEADPHONES. WHEN WEARING YOUR HEADPHONE RADIO, CARE MUST BE TAKEN WHEN YOU ARE ENGAGED IN ACTIVITIES WHERE YOUR SAFETY MIGHT BE ENDANGERED BY NOT HEARING OUTSIDE WARNINGS FROM HORNS, WHISTLES, SIRENS, ETC. *BE ESPECIALLY CAREFUL WHEN CROSSING STREETS.* PLEASE TAKE THE UTMOST CARE. YOU SHOULD ALSO ENSURE THAT CHILDREN WHO MIGHT BE USING YOUR RADIO ARE ADVISED OF THESE PRECAUTIONS.

_____ **1.** This radio requires two size C batteries.

_____ **2.** It does not matter how you put the headset on your head.

_____ **3.** This radio has two positions: FM and FM Stereo.

_____ **4.** This radio picks up AM stations.

_____ **5.** The balance control dial adjusts the volume of the headphones for each ear.

_____ **6.** This radio will automatically shut off when you remove the headphone plug from the headphone socket.

_____ **7.** The lead wire from the headphones acts as an FM antenna.

_____ **8.** The main safety problem in the use of the headphones is that they may prevent you from hearing outside sounds, especially horns, whistles, and sirens.

_____ **9.** If your set begins to work improperly, the first thing you should do is return it to the dealer for servicing.

_____ **10.** The clip at the back of the set is meant to attach the set to a belt or pocket.

Activity 4

Sequential directions — setting a digital watch

The directions in this activity tell you how to operate and set a digital display watch. First read the directions on the OPERATION of a digital watch. Then complete the chart that follows these directions.

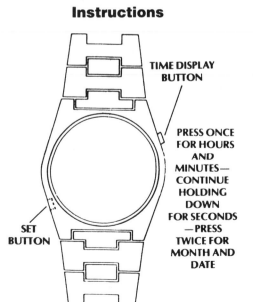

WH-5F-I
Instructions

TIME DISPLAY BUTTON

PRESS ONCE FOR HOURS AND MINUTES—CONTINUE HOLDING DOWN FOR SECONDS—PRESS TWICE FOR MONTH AND DATE

SET BUTTON

Operation

To display the time in hours and minutes, simply touch the TIME display button once. The hours and minutes will remain visible for a short period of time.

If the TIME display button is held down continuously, hours and minutes will disappear and a flashing seconds display will begin, remaining in view as long as the button is depressed.

To display month and date, simply press the TIME display button twice in rapid succession. A continuous display of month-date is available by holding the button down after the second push. Note that the month and date are separated by a dash (—), while hours and minutes are separated by a colon (:).

What will this watch display if you perform the steps in the following chart? Match each step with the correct result.

IF YOU...	YOUR WATCH WILL DISPLAY...		
	TIME HRS: MINUTES	FLASHING SECONDS	MONTH & DATE
1. Press the TIME display button once.			
2. Press the TIME display button and hold the button in depressed position.			
3. Depress the TIME display button twice.			
4. Push the TIME display button twice and hold the button down after the second push.			

Read the instructions for SETTING this watch. Then put the steps for setting the month, date, hour, and minute in the proper sequence.

Setting instructions

The SET button is used to select specific watch functions for setting. The TIME button is used for the actual setting operation. Pressing the SET button once (with a pointed object, such as a pencil or ball point pen) starts the month number flashing, signifying that the month can be set. Pressing it again enables you to set the date; the third time, the hour; the fourth, minutes and the fifth, normal operation. Note that the SET button operates sequentially. You can always tell which "set mode" your watch is in by observing the position of the flashing digits and noting whether a dash or a colon is displayed. The following table illustrates the SET button cycle.

ACTION	SET MODE	FLASHING DISPL.
Press once	Month	11 —
Press twice	Date	— 17
Press 3 times	Hours	5 :
Press 4 times	Minutes	: 46
Press 5 times	Normal	None

Setting the month

Press the SET button once and the month number will start flashing. The watch is now in its "month set mode." To change the month, simply hold the TIME button down and the month number will begin to advance. When the desired number flashes into view, release the TIME button. The correct month is now set into your watch.

_____ Press the SET button once.

_____ Release the TIME button when the number of the desired month appears.

_____ Hold the TIME button down.

_____ Look for a flashing month number indicating you are in the "month set mode."

Setting the date

Press the SET button a second time and the date will begin to flash, indicating that the watch is in its "date set mode." To change the date, press the TIME button and hold it down until the correct number appears. Your watch is programmed to adjust itself automatically for 29, 30 and 31 day months. It is only necessary to advance the date manually on the day following February 28 during non-leap years. To do this, select the "date set mode" and change the date from "29" to "1" (the month will advance automatically).

_____ Press the SET button a second time.

_____ Release the TIME button when the correct date appears.

_____ Hold the TIME button down.

_____ Look for a flashing date indicating you are in the "date set mode."

Setting hours

Press the SET button a third time. Hours will begin to flash, indicating the "hours set mode." To change hours, press the TIME button until the desired hour is displayed. In doing this, however, it is important to recognize the difference between a.m. hours and p.m. hours. If your watch is set to a.m. hours, the colon will include a dash (÷). During p.m. hours, the dash disappears (:). (If you have set your watch correctly during morning hours but the dash is absent, you must advance the hour setting through 12 more hours. By observing this a.m./p.m. difference, your watch will properly change date at midnight rather than at noon. Setting hours does not affect minutes, consequently, you can adjust your watch for time zone or daylight savings time changes without changing minutes.)

_____ Press the SET button a third time.

_____ Release the TIME button when the correct hour is displayed.

_____ Hold the TIME button.

_____ Look for a flashing hour indicating you are in the "hours set mode."

Setting minutes

Press the SET button a fourth time and minutes will start to flash, indicating the "minutes set mode." If you are not interested in setting your watch to the exact second, simply press the TIME button until the correct minute appears.

_____ Press the SET button a fourth time.

_____ Release the TIME button when the correct minute appears.

_____ Hold the TIME button down.

_____ Look for a flashing minute indicating you are in the "minute set mode."

CHECK YOUR UNDERSTANDING OF READING DIRECTIONS

Here are some words a person should know when following directions. Choose the correct word or words for the following sentences.

assemble   abrasive   peak performance

sequence   immerse

1. The instructions with my electric coffeemaker say not to _____ the base in water.

2. To set my digital watch, I must follow the instructions in exact _____ .

3. Some items come with many parts. It is important to follow the instructions exactly

to _____ them properly.

4. Some instructions warn against using _____ cleansers on a product.

5. I want to get _____ from my new tape deck.

Find the phrase that correctly completes each sentence.

_____ **6.** The most important task you must do when following directions is
a. to get someone to work with you.
b. to follow the directions in the correct order.
c. to work as rapidly as you can.

_____ **7.** Some directions warn against using certain kinds of cleansers. Usually the warnings are against using cleansers that
a. are not strong enough to do the job.
b. are liquids.
c. will scratch or damage the item.

_____ **8.** Using the wrong sequence when you try to assemble something probably means that
a. the item will be damaged.
b. the instructions don't matter anyway.
c. you will lose some of the parts.

_____ **9.** Digital watches must be set to show the correct time. The best way to do this is
a. to ask a friend to show you how to do it.
b. try out various ways of doing it until you get it right.
c. read and follow the directions for your particular watch.

_____ **10.** The words "do not immerse in water" are found on many directions and instructions. These words mean
a. do not wash.
b. do not use for cooking.
c. do not cover with water.

Reading recipes

WORDS TO KNOW

blend to combine two or more ingredients

briskly swiftly, with energy

combine mix together

container something to put food in, such as a jar or bowl

cream to mash or beat until smooth

dash a very small amount

fold mix in gently, without stirring

grate to shred with a grater

ingredients anything that goes into a recipe

preheat set oven temperature in advance

reduce lessen, as in turn down heat or allow liquid to boil away

scald to heat to just below the boiling point

simmer to cook in liquid at low heat on top of stove

yield the amount produced

yolk the yellow part of an egg

c. cup

doz. dozen (12)

gal. gallon (128 fluid ounces)

lb. pound (16 ounces)

lrg. large

min. minute

oz. ounce

pkg. package

pt. pint (16 fluid ounces)

qt. quart (32 fluid ounces)

sm. small

sq. square

tbsp. tablespoon

tsp. or t. teaspoon

Recipes have special words of their own. In recipes you will find words and abbreviations you do not use every day. These words and abbreviations tell you how to add ingredients. They tell you what the right measurements are and how long to cook a dish. They list the cooking temperature. The recipe words and abbreviations given above are the ones you will see most often.

Reading a recipe correctly can mean the difference between a good dish and a bad one. In addition to knowing what the words and abbreviations mean, you must be able to follow directions. Most recipes first give you a list of the ingredients you will need. They then tell you step-by-step what you should do to make the dish. Good cooks almost always use recipes.

Activity 5

Understanding recipe vocabulary

Match the words in column A with the definitions in column B.

	A		B
____ 1.	combine	a.	yellow part of the egg
____ 2.	briskly	b.	lessen; turn down
____ 3.	yolk	c.	mix together
____ 4.	container	d.	something to put food in
____ 5.	yield	e.	swiftly
____ 6.	reduce	f.	the amount produced

Activity 6

Understanding recipe abbreviations

Write the correct abbreviation beside each word.

1. ounce _____
2. cup _____
3. gallon _____
4. pound _____
5. tablespoon _____
6. quart _____
7. teaspoon _____

8. dozen _____
9. small _____
10. pint _____
11. package _____
12. square _____
13. large _____
14. minute _____

Following recipe directions

The illustration below points out the basic parts of a recipe. Study it carefully before doing the activities that follow.

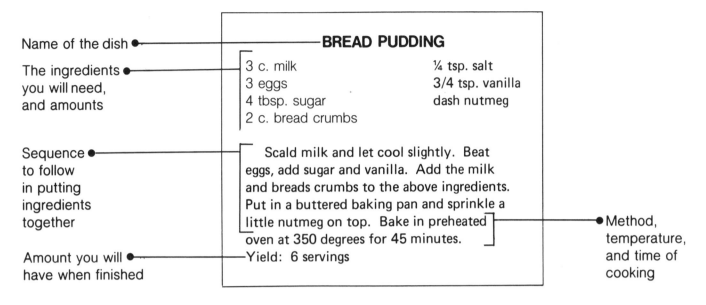

Name of the dish •————— **BREAD PUDDING**

The ingredients • you will need, and amounts

3 c. milk	¼ tsp. salt
3 eggs	3/4 tsp. vanilla
4 tbsp. sugar	dash nutmeg
2 c. bread crumbs	

Sequence • to follow in putting ingredients together

Scald milk and let cool slightly. Beat eggs, add sugar and vanilla. Add the milk and breads crumbs to the above ingredients. Put in a buttered baking pan and sprinkle a little nutmeg on top. Bake in preheated oven at 350 degrees for 45 minutes.

• Method, temperature, and time of cooking

Amount you will • have when finished

Yield: 6 servings

Activity 7

Reading recipe directions

Read the following recipes. Complete the statements about each recipe.

POUND CAKE

½ lb. butter	½ t. baking powder
1/3 c. shortening	½ t. salt
3 c. sugar	1 c. milk
5 eggs	1 t. vanilla
3 c. sifted flour	

Cream butter, shortening and sugar. Add eggs one at a time, beating after each addition. Add sifted dry ingredients, and milk alternately, beginning and ending with dry ingredients. Add vanilla flavoring. Bake in tube pan at 350 degrees for 1 hour and 30 minutes. Start in cold oven. Yield: 15 servings.

1. _____ butter is needed for this cake.

2. _____ eggs should be added _____ .

3. A _____ pan should be used for this cake.

4. The cake should cook _____ at a temperature of _____ .

5. The cake will serve _____ people.

6. The oven should be _____ at the beginning of cooking.

VEG-A-BURGER

1 lb. hamburger
½ c. onions
1 8-oz can tomato sauce
3/4 c. water
1 c. canned green beans, drained
1 c. uncooked rice
1 c. whole kernel corn, drained
1 c. tomato catsup

    Brown hamburger and onions in pan; add tomato sauce and water. Add green beans, rice, and corn. Heat to simmer; add catsup. Cook until rice is tender, about 30 minutes. Yield: 6 servings.

1. One _____ of tomato sauce is needed for this dish.

2. One _____ of tomato catsup is used.

3. The rice should be _____ when it is added.

4. The whole kernel corn should be _____ .

5. Brown _____ and _____ in a pan.

6. This dish will serve _____ people.

Activity 8

Reading recipe directions

Read the recipes below. Then read the sets of directions below each recipe. Decide which directions are written in the proper order.

LEMON SPONGE PIE

4 tbsp. butter or margarine, softened
1¼ c. sugar
4 eggs, separated
3 tbsp. flour
dash of salt
1¼ c. milk
grated peel of 1 lemon
¼ c. lemon juice
1 unbaked 9-inch pie shell

Use large bowl and spoon or mixer to cream together butter and sugar until fluffy. Beat in yolks of eggs, flour, salt, milk, lemon peel, and juice. Use a small bowl with clean beaters to beat egg whites until stiff but not dry. Fold into milk mixture. Pour into pie shell. Bake in preheated 375° oven 20 minutes; reduce heat to 300° and bake 40 minutes longer or until top is golden and toothpick inserted in center comes out dry. Cool on rack. Yields 8 slices.

_____ **1.** Beat in egg yolks, flour, salt, milk, lemon peel, and juice.
Cream together butter and sugar until fluffy.
Beat egg whites until stiff.

_____ **2.** Cream together butter and sugar until fluffy.
Beat in egg yolks, flour, salt, milk, lemon peel, and juice.
Beat egg whites until stiff.

_____ **3.** Beat egg whites until stiff.
Cream together butter and sugar until fluffy.
Beat in egg yolks, flour, salt, milk, lemon peel, and juice.

_____ **4.** Pour into pie shell.
Fold into milk mixture.
Bake in preheated oven.

_____ **5.** Bake in preheated oven.
Pour into pie shell.
Fold into milk mixture.

_____ **6.** Fold into milk mixture.
Pour into pie shell.
Bake in preheated oven.

PIZZA

1 Pizza Dough recipe
cooking oil
1 8-oz. can tomato sauce
1 6-oz. can tomato paste
1 large clove garlic, crushed
2 tsp. sugar
1 tsp. oregano
¾ tsp. basil
½ tsp. crushed red pepper

¼ lb. sweet Italian sausage (skin removed) or
   pork sausage meat, browned and drained
1/8 lb. pepperoni, sliced thin
¼ c. mushrooms, thinly sliced
½ c. chopped onion
½ c. chopped green pepper
½ to 1 can (about 2 oz.) anchovy fillets,
   drained.
½ lb. mozzarella cheese, shredded
¼ c. grated Parmesan cheese

Prepare dough as directed. Then gently stretch or roll out dough to fit greased 16-inch pizza pan (or divide dough in half and form two 12-inch circles; place on greased cookie sheets). Crimp edges to form rim. Brush dough with oil. Bake (without toppings) on lowest oven rack in preheated 450° oven 3 to 4 minutes or until crust bottom is slightly golden. Meanwhile, mix tomato sauce and paste, garlic, sugar, oregano, basil, and red pepper. Spread evenly over crust. Top with sausage, pepperoni, mushrooms, onion, green pepper, and anchovies. Bake 15 minutes, then sprinkle with mozzarella and Parmesan. Bake 8 to 10 minutes or until cheese is melted with golden crust. Makes 4 servings.

Which sets of directions are in the proper order?

_____ **1.** Brush dough with oil.
Crimp edges to form rim.
Roll out dough to fit pan.

_____ **2.** Crimp edges to form rim.
Roll out dough to fit pan.
Brush dough with oil.

_____ **3.** Roll out dough to fit pan.
Crimp edges to form rim.
Brush dough with oil.

_____ **4.** Mix tomato sauce and paste, garlic, sugar, oregano, basil, and red pepper.
Spread evenly over crust.
Top with sausage, pepperoni, mushrooms, onion, green pepper, and anchovies.

_____ **5.** Top with sausage, pepperoni, mushrooms, onion, green pepper, and anchovies.
Spread evenly over crust.
Mix tomato sauce and paste, garlic, sugar, oregano, basil, and red pepper.

_____ **6.** Spread evenly over crust.
Top with sausage, pepperoni, mushrooms, onion, green pepper, and anchovies.
Mix tomato sauce and paste, garlic, sugar, oregano, basil, and red pepper.

CHECK YOUR UNDERSTANDING OF RECIPES

Here are some of the most important abbreviations a person must know to read a recipe correctly. Write the full word for each abbreviation given below.

1. c. _____

2. tsp. _____

3. qt. _____

4. t. _____

5. sm. _____

6. gal. _____

7. doz. _____

8. lb. _____

9. tbsp. _____

10. pt. _____

Here are some of the most important "how to" words used in reading recipes. Write out a definition for each word.

11. preheat _____

12. cream _____

13. grate _____

14. scald _____

15. simmer _____

Taking tests

WORDS TO KNOW

accurate   correct, without mistake

ACT   American College Test; test often required before entering college

applicant   person applying for a job

answer grid   evenly spaced boxes or lines for marking answers to test questions

essay question   a question that requires the writer to explain his or her thoughts

horizontal line   a line that runs across a page

performance test   a test that requires the person to perform a task, such as typing, or using tools

SAT   Scholastic Aptitude Test; test often required before entering college

tester   person giving the test

vertical line   a line that runs up and down a page

multiple-choice question   a question that lists a number of possible answers

Tests are designed to measure both skills and knowledge. They are given in schools and for qualifying for jobs. They require following directions carefully. Tests are also used to determine which colleges you qualify for and, sometimes, the courses you will take. Perhaps you are familiar with the ACT and SAT tests.

Tests can take many different forms. Performance tests ask you to work with tools or objects to demonstrate your skill. You may also have to put something together. Other tests are oral or mechanized. You may be asked to listen to a tape and then respond on a machine or computer. Most tests, however, are "paper and pencil" tests.

Learning to take a paper and pencil test properly is a skill in itself. For example, you may know the answer to the question on a test, but you may not understand where and how to write your answer.

One form of paper and pencil test is the test *booklet*. For this type of test, you record your answer in a booklet or on the separate answer sheet that comes with the test booklet.

Test booklets

On the first page of a test booklet you are usually asked to identify yourself. There will be very specific questions aimed at you personally. You must answer these questions accurately because they tell the tester *who* you are.

On the following page are two examples of test booklet covers. They are for an employment test. The first example is marked "incorrect." It has not been filled out properly. The second example is marked "correct." The applicant has given all the information requested. The information is clear and complete. Take a moment to study these examples.

INCORRECT

The applicant ignored the first request on the form. He wrote in longhand instead of printing.

This line calls for "last" name first.

The applicant did not indicate if Cherrylawn was a street, avenue or what! And where is the city, state, and ZIP Code?

This line is incomplete. The year is omitted.

Miller has *printed* this entry. Perhaps he now realizes the form says "please print."

EMPLOYMENT TEST

(Please Print Clearly)

NAME _____
Last   First   Middle Name or Initial

ADDRESS _____
Street   City   State   Zip Code

DATE _____ 19 _____ S.S. _____

JOB YOU ARE APPLYING FOR __Mail Clerk__

HOW DID YOU HEAR ABOUT THIS JOB OPENING? (Please Check One Box)

☐ Newspaper Advertisement   ☐ Government Employment Service

☐ Employment Agency   ☐ An employee

☒ Other (Please Specify) _____

This applicant has not indicated exactly how he learned about this job. The form said "specify."

Miller's social security number should have gone here.

CORRECT

Applicant *printed* all information.

Applicant gave his name in the order requested— *last name first.*

The applicant wrote "Cherrylawn" *Street.* The city, state, and ZIP Code are given.

The *date is complete*— September 10, 1989.

EMPLOYMENT TEST

(Please Print Clearly)

NAME __Miller__   __John__   __V.__
Last   First   Middle Name or Initial

ADDRESS __1805 Cherrylawn St., Amber, IL   60512__
Street   City   State   Zip Code

DATE __September 10__ 19 __89__ S.S. __234-56-8469__

JOB YOU ARE APPLYING FOR __Mail Clerk__

HOW DID YOU HEAR ABOUT THIS JOB OPENING? (Please Check One Box)

☐ Newspaper Advertisement   ☐ Government Employment Service

☐ Employment Agency   ☐ An employee

☒ Other (Please Specify) __School Guidance Counselor__

Applicant has *specified* how he heard about this job opening.

The applicant's *social security number is given.*

The personal information requested on test booklets should be *neat and complete*. In the first example, John V. Miller's handwriting is careless. If the tester needed to contact John, he or she might not be able to read John's name. Much of the information on this application was left incomplete. One item missing was John's social security number. Perhaps John did not know his social security number. Many people don't. John may not have known what "S.S. #" means. We know that this applicant *can* print. John's entry on the line "Job you are applying for" is *printed*. Although this entry is not very neat, it is printed. The tester should have no trouble reading it. The last incomplete entry had to do with specifying how John learned about this opening. In the second example we learn that the school guidance counselor told John about the job opening. This response should have gone in the first example.

Activity 9
Completing test booklet covers

Write out the information requested on the following test booklet cover. Use today's date. This is test form 2-B.

TROJAN MANUFACTURING COMPANY

Employment Test

Print clearly

Name _____
       Last   First   Middle

Address _____
         Street   City   State   Zip

Date of Test _____ 19_____

Form of Test (Check one box):

☐ 1-A   ☐ 2-A   ☐ 3-A
☐ 1-B   ☐ 2-B   ☐ 3-B

DO NOT OPEN TEST BOOKLET UNTIL TESTER INSTRUCTS YOU TO

Following directions on tests

Did you notice in the activity above that the applicant was asked *not* to open the test booklet? When you take tests, especially employment tests, you will be timed. A tester will tell you when to BEGIN a test and when to STOP. There will be directions with your booklet. For example, "DO NOT TURN THE PAGE UNTIL YOU ARE TOLD TO DO SO" or "WAIT FOR FURTHER INSTRUCTIONS." These directions *must* be followed. Many times you will take a test that not only measures *what* you know, but how *quickly* you can use your knowledge. This type of test is called a SPEED AND ACCURACY TEST. You must read and follow directions on a speed and accuracy test exactly. You must begin when the tester tells you to begin. You must stop when the tester tells you to stop. Because you are being timed, you must read and follow these directions quickly. But never begin this type of test without understanding exactly what you are to do.

Read the directions for the speed and accuracy test below. But DO NOT take the test.

SPEED AND ACCURACY TEST

This is a test of speed and accuracy for a job as a mail room clerk. In this test you will find names and numbers in pairs. If the two names or the two numbers of a pair are exactly the same, put a check (✔) on the line between them. If the two names or the two numbers are different, do nothing.

EXAMPLE

(1) 33155 __√__ 33155

(2) 45788 __√__ 45788

(3) Wayne Riley __√__ Wayne Riley

(4) Janet Martin _____ Janette Martin

Now answer the questions below. This is a SPEED AND ACCURACY TEST. Work as quickly as you can.

(1) 5234 _____ 5234

(2) 8807 _____ 8807

(3) 1243 _____ 1234

(4) 10007 _____ 1007

(5) Betty Marsh _____ Betty March

(6) 8813 _____ 8831

(7) 1080307 _____ 1080307

(8) Joyce Jackson _____ Joyce Jackson

(9) Clarence Saunders _____ Clarence Sanders

(10) Emma Whitaker _____ Emma Whitaker

Here are examples of how two applicants responded to this test:

(1) 5234 _____ 5234	(1) 5234 _✓_ 5234
(2) 8807 _____ 8807	(2) 8807 _✓_ 8807
(3) 1243 _✓_ 1234	(3) 1243 _____ 1234
(4) 10007 _✓_ 1007	(4) 10007 _____ 1007
(5) Betty Marsh _✓_ Betty March	(5) Betty Marsh _____ Betty March
(6) 8813 _✓_ 8831	(6) 8813 _____ 8831
(7) 1080307 _____ 1080307	(7) 1080307 _✓_ 1080307
(8) Joyce Jackson _____ Joyce Jackson	(8) Joyce Jackson _✓_ Joyce Jackson
(9) Clarence Saunders _✓_ Clarence Sanders	(9) Clarence Saunders _____ Clarence Sanders
(10) Emma Whitaker _____ Emma Whitaker	(10) Emma Whitaker _✓_ Emma Whitaker

The second applicant has checked the correct responses. The first applicant has checked all incorrect responses. The first applicant *thinks* he has checked all the right responses. Turn back to the original directions. See if you can determine where this applicant went wrong.

The first applicant misread the directions. The directions said "If the two names . . . are *exactly the same,* put a check (✔) on the line. . . . If the two names . . . are *different, do nothing.*" The first applicant read these directions too quickly. He was sure that he would be asked to do nothing when the names or numbers were the same. As a result of this thinking, all of his answers are wrong. If you do not follow the directions on a speed and accuracy test, you could fail the test completely.

Activity 10

Following test directions

Read the test directions for the speed and accuracy test below. Then answer the questions just as you would if you were actually being tested. You will *not* be timed for this practice activity. But you should pretend this is an actual test and work as fast as you can.

SPEED AND ACCURACY TEST

Directions

This is a test of speed and accuracy in one type of clerical work. In this test there are pairs of names and pairs of numbers. If the two names or the two numbers of a pair are *exactly the same,* make a check mark on the line. If they are different, make no mark on that line.

Look at the four examples, A, B, C, and D, that have been done correctly. In example A, the two numbers are different, so no check mark was made on the line between them. In example B, the numbers are exactly the same so a check mark was made on the line between them. Now look at examples C and D.

A. 3315 _____ 3135   C. Jim Battle _____ John Battle

B. 45782 _✓_ 45782   D. Bill Evans _✓_ Bill Evans

Numbers			Names	
1. 4721 ___ 4721			**6.** Louis Eldern	___ Louis Eldern
2. 584 ___ 584			**7.** James Meyer	___ James Mayer
3. 80962 ___ 90862			**8.** Arthur Lungren	___ Arthur Lundgren
4. 9325 ___ 9325			**9.** Frank Schaefer	___ Frank Schaefer
5. 0365 ___ 0356			**10.** Allan Kenmore	___ Albert Kenmore

Activity 11

Following test directions

In this activity you will take a test. You are to read and follow the directions for the test. *You will not be timed.* This activity will give you practice in following test directions.

VOCABULARY TEST

Directions

This is a test of the meanings of words.

Look at the word HURRY, and the four words that follow it.

One of the words—rush—means about the same thing as HURRY, so a check mark has been put on the line next to the word *rush.*

HURRY   move ___   rush ✓   shout ___   walk ___

Below are words printed in capital letters. To the right of each of these words are four more words—like the example shown above. Put a check mark on the line next to the *one* word that means most nearly the same thing as the word printed in capital letters.

Answer each question, but do not spend too much time on any one question.

If you are not sure of the answer, guess.

VOCABULARY TEST

1. SAVE   part ___   keep ___   spend ___   sort ___

2. STAY   remain ___ result ___   leave ___   press ___

3. IDEA   story ___   value ___   thought ___ subject ___

4. GATHER   collect ___ choose ___ remove ___ decide ___

5. HIRE   raise ___   locate ___   divide ___   employ ___

6. NEARLY   every ___   quickly ___ almost ___ never ___

Using test booklets with separate answer sheets

Many test booklets come with separate answer sheets. Filling in an answer sheet correctly is important. Part of your answer sheet will be for "gridding in" your name. Did Kevin Abraham grid in the answer sheet below correctly?

First name starts here

STUDENT'S NAME
Print last name, one letter per box. Skip a box. Print first name. Darken appropriate circle below each letter. Darken top circles under boxes which do not contain letters.

| A | B | R | A | H | A | M | | K | E | V | I | N | | | |

1. Fill in your name, one letter per box. Notice that the last name is called for first.

2. The rows under each box contain the alphabet. Go down the row and find the letter in the box at the top of the row.

3. Darken that letter and do the same for each box that has a letter in it. This is called "gridding in."

Note—If your name has more letters than there are boxes, fill in as much of your name as you can and leave the rest of it off.

This section of the answer sheet is for you to fill in additional information about yourself.

1. Mark your I.D. number

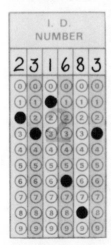

2. Mark the month and year you were born

BIRTH DATE	
MONTH	YEAR
JAN. ○	(Last 2 digits)
FEB. ○	
MAR. ●	⓪ ⓪
APR. ○	① ①
MAY ○	② ②
JUN. ○	③ ●
JUL. ○	④ ④
AUG. ○	⑤ ⑤
SEP. ○	⑥ ⑥
OCT. ○	● ⑦
NOV. ○	⑧ ⑧
DEC. ○	⑨ ⑨

3. Show whether you are male or female

4. Show which test form you are using

Responding on separate answer sheets

When you are asked to answer test questions on a separate sheet, you will usually be given a grid sheet for your answers. Grids may be horizontal. They may also be vertical, or up-and-down grids.

Beside each question in a test booklet will be a number. The same numbers will appear on the answer sheet. Spaces opposite the number will match the question on the answer sheet. You must always be sure you mark your answer in the space with the same number as the question in the test booklet. You must also mark answers as directed. Study this sample from an answer sheet:

Marking the answer sheet

1. When is Independence Day?
   A. May 31
   B. June 1
   C. July 4
   D. December 25

The answer blacked in on the answer sheet is correct—C, July 4.

When marking an answer sheet, remember—
1. Shade in the section you have selected for your response and *only that section.*
2. Stray marks on the answer sheet may be counted as incorrect answers by the scoring machine.
3. If you must erase, erase a mark *completely.*
4. Always be sure the number of the question on the answer sheet corresponds to the number in the test booklet.

Multiple-choice questions

The questions on the test in Activity 12 are multiple-choice questions. Multiple-choice questions are the most widely used type of test question. Of course, you will not always know the correct answer to a multiple-choice question. Many times, though, you can use the process of elimination to determine the correct response. Although some questions do not lend themselves to guessing, many do. Guess by eliminating wrong answers until you are left with one possible answer.

When answering a multiple-choice question, read the question carefully, especially the first part. Your complete understanding of the question is very important. Try the process of elimination. For example, you may not know who wrote *Gulliver's Travels,* but you may know who didn't.

Question: Who wrote *Gulliver's Travels?*
A. George Washington
B. Eli Whitney
C. Mark Twain
D. Jonathan Swift

You probably know that "D" is the correct response even if you never heard of Jonathan Swift. First, you can eliminate George Washington. He is well known as our first President and for chopping down the cherry tree but not for being a writer. Eli Whitney invented the cotton gin. And you know that when you studied Mark Twain in English class, all of the stories you read were about Tom Sawyer, Huck Finn, and the Mississippi River. So you arrive at Jonathan Swift through the process of elimination.

When you use reason—or plain common sense—to answer a multiple-choice question, look for words and phrases that are clues to the answer—

always	the only	except	sometimes
never	chief	but	one
least	main	or	usually
highest	near	not	best

Always consider how these words and phrases can influence a question. For example, this simple question is difficult to answer.

The reason for the high school drop-out rate is
A. economics
B. outside interests
C. boredom
D. low success in school

Watch how key words and phrases can narrow down the possible responses to this question:

The reason for the high school drop-out rate is *usually* . . .

The *main* reason for the high school drop-out rate is . . .

One of the least important reasons for the high school drop-out rate is . . .

What do you feel is the correct (best) response to this multiple-choice question?

A small independent merchant has the best chance to compete with large chain stores by
A. buying in quantity
B. hiring more expert management
C. manufacturing and selling his own items
D. offering more personalized service

"A" certainly could not be the best way for the merchant to compete with large chains. A small merchant would not have the money or space to buy in large quantities. Although "B" would improve any business, it is not likely that it would increase business enough for the merchant to be competitive with chain stores. Remember, the question asks for the "best chance." Response "C" is not even a realistic choice. Most independent merchants do not have the ability to manufacture items. The correct response is "D." This is the only area where a small merchant may have an advantage over a large chain. Because a business is small, it has the ability to give customers personal services chain stores cannot provide.

All of the choices were possible to some extent. By using an intelligent process of reasoning and by identifying key phrases, you can answer many multiple-choice questions correctly.

Activity 12

Answering multiple-choice questions

This activity gives you practice in responding to multiple-choice questions. Answer each question on the information test by writing down the letter of the correct answer.

INFORMATION TEST

QUESTION BOOKLET

_____ **1.** What is the capital of the United States?

    A. Washington, D.C.
    B. New York
    C. Philadelphia
    D. Chicago

_____ **2.** When is Independence Day?

    A. May 31
    B. December 25
    C. July 4
    D. February 22

_____ **3.** Which of these cities has the largest population?

    A. New York
    B. Chicago
    C. San Francisco
    D. Philadelphia

_____ **4.** The President of the United States is elected for a term of

    A. four years.
    B. two years.
    C. ten years.
    D. six years.

_____ **5.** Where does the United States launch space flights?

    A. Cape Hatteras
    B. Cape May
    C. Cape Cod
    D. Cape Kennedy

Test taking tips

Review these TIPS on TEST TAKING. They may help you.

1. Determine a pace for the test you are taking. If you are allowed to look over the entire test before answering any questions, you should. This will give you an idea of how quickly you must work. It's a good idea to wear a watch the day of a test because test sections are often timed.

2. Always work as quickly as you can, but try to answer all questions carefully.
3. You may find it to your advantage to skip a difficult question and go back to it later.
4. On some tests, you can guess at an answer when you are not sure of the correct response. But on other tests, you are penalized for wrong answers. On this type of test, it is better to have *no answer* than a wrong answer. Be sure about these rules before you start the test.
5. The best guess is the one that comes from the process of elimination. Too many wild guesses can hurt your score.
6. Remember to use reasoning on multiple-choice questions. Always look for key words like "always," "most," and "never." These words help narrow down the *best* response.
7. And remember, you must read and follow all directions carefully. If you misread the directions on a test, all your answers could be wrong.

CHECK YOUR UNDERSTANDING OF TAKING TESTS

Here are some words you should know about tests. On your paper write the correct word or phrase for each of the following sentences.

| multiple-choice | SAT | tester |
| horizontal | applicant | vertical |

1. As a job _____ you may be asked to take an employment test.

2. Be sure to follow the directions given by the _____ when you are taking a test.

3. Test questions with a choice of three or more answers are called _____ questions.

4. Sometimes test answer grids have boxes with lines that run across the page. These are called _____ boxes.

5. Many colleges ask for _____ scores to be attached to the college application form.

6. _____ answer grids run up and down the page.

Decide whether each of the following statements is TRUE (T) or FALSE (F).

_____ **7.** If you are allowed, you should look over the entire test before answering any questions.

_____ **8.** Sometimes it is an advantage to skip a hard question and go back to it later.

_____ **9.** Wild guesses can never hurt your score on a test.

_____ **10.** Key words like "always," "most," and "never" can help you choose the best multiple-choice answer.

Reading newspapers

One of the best places to learn about events is your newspaper. It gives you the local, national, and world news. It also gives you entertainment, sports, and travel news.

Reading a newspaper is a good way to spend time. A newspaper gives you information on many subjects. In this section, you will study the parts of a newspaper. You will read news stories and editorials. You will read for both facts and opinions. You will also practice using the classified ads. Most emphasis will be on help-wanted ads. The help-wanted ads are a good way to get information about jobs.

The sections of a newspaper

WORDS TO KNOW

alphabetical   arranged in the order of the letters of the alphabet

classified ads   advertisements for jobs, items for sale, etc., arranged by subject

editorial   a written comment on current events that gives the opinion of the newspaper's editor or publisher

features   articles about special subjects, such as food or travel

financial   having to do with money

horoscope   a chart that uses the positions of planets and signs of the Zodiac to predict the future

index   a list of items with page numbers, usually arranged alphabetically

obituary   notice of a person's death

real estate   buildings and land

Newspapers have many sections. By creating different sections, papers make information easy to find. For example, you can quickly turn to the sports section for the score of last night's football game. In the entertainment sections you can find the time of the movie you want to see. Almost all newspapers have these sections:

Business	Editorials	News
Classified ads	Entertainment	Sports
Comics	Fashion	TV guide
Death notices	Home	Weather

47

Newspaper indexes

Most newspapers have an index. The index tells you where to find the type of information you want.

Index to the newspaper

Subjects arranged alphabetically

Accent	(1-12)F
Bridge	14D
Business	3C
Classified	4-20C
Comics	14, 15D
Contact 10	16B
Crossword	15D
Death notices	11C
Editorial/Opinion	18, 19A
Entertainment	12, 13D
Finance	3C
Horoscope	14D
Kitchen Talk	1-20E
Movie guide	4C
Obituaries	11C
Sports	1-11D
Stock tables	3C
TV	8, 9E
Wonderworld	15D

Page numbers for this subject

Section of the newspaper (each section begins with page 1)

Activity 1

Using the newspaper index

Look at topics 1-10 below. Which index headings will help you find the topics? List the number of each topic beside the correct heading.

1. A restaurant guide
2. Sewing tips
3. Movies in your neighborhood
4. The leader in the baseball pennant race
5. Yesterday's football scores

6. Program on Channel 7 at 8 P.M.
7. Opinions on current issues
8. Night club shows
9. Apartments for rent
10. Recipes

Index Heading

Sports _____

Editorial _____

Classified ads _____

Entertainment _____

Home section _____

Activity 2

Using the newspaper index

Complete the chart below about this newspaper index.

Accent............................. 1-20	Editorial/Opinion........... 18, 19A
Art 4M	Finance 1-6E
Books...............................2M	Hobbies 5J
Bridge...............................5J	Homes/Gardens 1, 2L
Business 1-6E	Horoscope 19C
Camera 9M	Lively Arts 1-10M
CB Radio............................8M	Movie guide 6M
Classified........................1-8F, 1-8G	Obituaries......................... 19C
Comics 2-8L	Sports.......................... 1-12D
Contact 10.........................1B	Stock tables.....................3-6E
Crossword 8K	Travel 1-6J
Death notices 19C	

Topics	Pages	Section
How to grow house plants		
Tours to Las Vegas		
What's in store for a Gemini today		
Stamp collecting		
Job openings		
Your favorite comic strip		
Stock averages		

Getting information from news stories

A news story gives you the facts about current events. After reading a news story, you should be able to answer questions about a news event. Usually a news story will answer who, what, when, and where. Sometimes a story will tell how and why something happened.

Activity 3

Reading news stories

Read these news stories and answer the questions that follow each story.

Girls don't lag in math, study finds

By Jon Van

GIRLS ARE JUST as good as boys are at learning difficult mathematics, according to a study by University of Chicago researchers.

The study contradicts a Johns Hopkins University report that concluded that boys are inherently better than girls at mathematical reasoning.

"There just is no difference at all between the ability of boys and girls to learn mathematics," said Zalman Usiskin, associate professor of education at the University of Chicago.

Usiskin and two colleagues, Sharon Senk and Roberta Dees, tested 1,366 high school students in classrooms across the country to measure their ability to write proofs for geometry problems. It was the first large-scale test of geometry proof ability ever undertaken in the United States.

"Writing these proofs involves the highest order of thinking in high school mathematics," Usiskin said. "We found that in some areas the girls did better and in other areas the boys did, but there were no consistent differences that could be explained by sex."

THE RESULTS directly contradict a study by J.C. Stanley and C.P. Benbow of Johns Hopkins that was given widespread publicity a few years ago, Usiskin said.

In that study, exceptionally bright children in the 6th and 7th grades were given high school level Scholastic Aptitude Tests, and the boys scored better in mathematics than the girls.

Those tests required a knowledge of high school algebra that neither the boys nor the girls had learned in school, Usiskin said. The fact that boys did better than girls may mean they learned more math outside of class than the girls, but it doesn't prove a genetic difference, he said.

"There was nothing genetic in the Hopkins study, and we felt they were going a little far on the basis of test scores alone to suggest a genetic difference between the sexes," Usiskin said.

THE UNIVERSITY of Chicago study tested pupils over material they had been taught in school.

"If boys and girls are in the same class, exposed to the same material, there is no difference in their ability to learn mathematics," Usiskin said.

1. What is the main subject of this article? _____

2. What was done? _____

3. Why was it done? _____

4. How was it done? _____

5. Where was it done? _____

6. How many high school students were tested for this study? _____

7. Were the boys and girls in this study tested separately? _____

8. What is the name of the test that was given to 6th and 7th grade students in a study done a few years

   ago? _____

9. What are the names of the three people who did the most recent study? _____

   _____

10. Were students in the most recent study tested in algebra or in geometry? _____

Pupils go to mat in Academic Olympics

By Casey Banas
Education editor

NINE-YEAR-OLD Carl Jones normally kneels at his beside, says his prayers, climbs into bed and falls fast asleep, but his nightly routine has been different during the last four weeks.

He still recites his prayers without fail, but then reaches under his pillow for a piece of paper and goes to work. "I put my poem under my pillow so I could memorize it," he said.

On Tuesday, his bedtime efforts paid off as Carl became a champion in the District 9 Academic Olympics. He is a 4th grader at Dodge Elementary School, 2651 W. Washington Blvd., and he was the school's representative in the oratory contest, one area of competition among 20 elementary schools in the West Side district.

Standing perhaps two whiskers higher than 3 feet and weighing about 40 pounds, little Carl seemed like a speck on the auditorium stage of Crane High School, 2245 W. Jackson Blvd.

BUT HE WAS dynamite and the jam-packed crowd of 600 children and adults applauded thunderously when Carl finished a spirited recital, complete with extensive gestures, of Lucille Clifton's poem about black pride, "Black B C's."
He began:

A is for Africa land of sun
The king of continents the ancient one
B is for books where readers find
Treasures for heart and mind
C is for cowboys king of the West
Black men were some of the best

And he ended:

Z is for zenith highest, top
The place for us and there we'll stop

Carl was one of more than 200 youngsters, winners in local school contests, who battled for medals in oratory, math, essay, and quiz competitions as other classmates cheered them on in an atmosphere usually experienced at athletic events.

THE EDUCATORS, seeking to replicate some of the classic rituals of the Olympic games, started the competition with a parade of school banners into the auditorium. Earlean Lindsey, the district council president, carried a torch.

After various events, officials slipped medals around the necks of the champions and runners-up, who stood on pedestals denoting first-, second- and third-place finishes.

The Academic Olympics is not the brainchild of Board of Education members or the superintendent of schools but of inner-city administrators, principals, and teachers who want to elevate the achievements levels of their pupils. They turned to an old-fashioned remedy: Academic competition among schools.

Preston Bryant, superintendent of District 10 on the West Side, started the grass-roots move three years ago with the first districtwide Academic Olympics among elementary schools under his jurisdiction.

"WE SAW a need for encouraging our youngsters to look toward academic instead of sports areas," Bryant said. "It also gave teachers added emphasis and gusto to teach the curriculum."

Now the Academic Olympics idea has spread to seven inner-city districts—Districts 7, 8, 9, 10, 11, 13 and 14 on the West, Near West and South Sides. Each district is having its own competition this month, and on June 1 and 2 there will be a "challenge of champions" for winners from the seven districts at Young High School.

The children and their teachers have worked for weeks to prepare for the competition, putting in scores of hours of their own time in studying math, literature, science, social studies, art and music.

They were kids like Valencia Murray, a 6th grader at Skinner Elementary School, 111 S. Throop St., who admitted she was nervous but said, "I read more science and social studies books at home to prepare for this."

VALENCIA WAS one of five members of her school's "Academic Bowl" and had to be ready to answer in an instant questions on any elementary school subject. The "Academic Bowl" is reminiscent of the old television "College Bowl" show when teams of college students had to answer questions in a flash.

Nine schools competed Tuesday in a semifinal round. The pupils from Gladstone Elementary, 1231 S. Damen Ave., led the way with 225 points as Everette Lowe, an 8th grader, repeatedly came up with instant correct answers to questions such as: "What is conversation between characters called in a short story or novel?" ["Dialogue."] "Who was the first black to sing in the Metropolitan Opera?" ["Marian Anderson."] "What age must a person attain in order to become President of the United States?" [35.] "What are old Egyptian picture writings called?" ["Hieroglyphics."]

Moments after leading his team off the stage, Lowe said:

"I'm relieved and very happy. I was cold all over. My heart was pounding. We came to school early every morning and we were drilled again and again."

He and other Gladstone team members were quick to praise their teacher and coach, Virginia Dow, for her efforts in training them.

Roger Heaps, instructional coordinator for District 9 and quizmaster for the "Academic Bowl," observed:

"See how the kids really get into it? The participants here will go back to their schools and tell others how exciting it is. This will generate more interest next year. But I only wish we would be able to film the competition and show children in schools so they could see the excitement."

1. Who is Carl Jones? _____

2. What did he do? _____

3. Where was the Academic Olympics held? _____

4. Why did educators create the Academic Olympics? _____

5. Where in the city did these educators teach? _____

Editorials The newspaper has an opinion section called the editorial page. On this page the editors write their ideas and opinions on news topics. Sometimes the publisher of a newspaper will comment on a current issue or news event. Some newspapers also ask their readers to write in with their opinions.

Below is a sample editorial. A local newspaper is giving its opinion on an issue that affects its readers.

Interstate Tunnel Detours Important

Commercial trucking firms hauling hazardous cargoes are likely to look on interstate highway detours as an expensive, time-consuming nuisance.

There are two such detours on Interstate 77 — one at the East River Mountain tunnel on the West Virginia-Virginia state line, and a second at the Big Walker Mountain tunnel in Virginia.

But these two particular detours serve a very important purpose — they route hazardous traffic — such as gasoline and high explosives — around the tunnels, thereby helping to reduce the chance of an accident which could result in fatality-causing explosions and heavy damage or destruction of the tunnels, both of which are about a mile long. Unfortunately, no such restrictions apply to a third tunnel on I-77 — the one on the West Virginia Turnpike section of I-77.

Last week's tanker truck explosion which followed a collision with a bus in an Oakland, Calif. highway tunnel proves just how important detours for hazardous cargoes can be.

The tanker truck, loaded with more than 8,000 gallons of gasoline, blew up in the tunnel, creating a 1,000-degree inferno that melted vehicles in seconds and incinerated their occupants. Six people were known dead.

Spilling gasoline ignited and flashed into a fireball that in seconds roared through about a third of the half-mile-long tunnel, melting brass fittings, popping tiles from the walls, and turning a 2-inch-thick concrete lining into sooty powder.

If such an accident ever occurred in one of the three tunnels on Interstate I-77, the resulting damage could effectively block through traffic for months or years, rendering partially ineffective one of this state's two major north-south highways.

West Virginia and Virginia have too much invested in their high-cost interstates to let this happen. The detour regulation is a good one.

In this editorial the paper lists some of the dangers of driving hazardous cargoes through tunnels. The piece of writing has both facts and opinions. Unlike the news story, the facts are not just reported. They are used to back up the opinion. The whole editorial builds an argument *in favor of* highway detours.

An editorial should not be confused with a news story. News stories are reports. They give the who, what, when, and where of events. They give the facts as they happened. Although an editorial may use facts, it is an *opinion column.*

Activity 4

Editorials and news stories: "fact vs. opinion"

Read each statement below. Decide if the statement belongs in an editorial or in a news story.

1. Property taxes should not be the way to pay for schools. Editorial News Story

2. Thirty-four billion dollars in property taxes are used for schools each year. Editorial News Story

3. More freeways will bring more business to the downtown area. Editorial News Story

4. Two new freeways will be finished in 1985. Editorial News Story

5. If election days were changed to Saturdays instead of Tuesdays, more people would vote. Editorial News Story

6. There was a 65 percent voter turnout at the last election. Editorial News Story

7. Our town needs a new park on Main Street. Editorial News Story

8. The city council voted 9-6 in favor of building a park on Main Street. Editorial News Story

9. The last day of the school year is June 16. Editorial News Story

10. The present school calendar is inconvenient for many people. Editorial News Story

Activity 5

Answer the questions about the following editorial.

Reading editorials

The Roar Of Motorcycles

Raleigh County Sheriff Claude England has decided it is a waste of his deputies' time and his department's money to answer calls concerning disturbances by youngsters riding motorcycles.

Even if a deputy can catch a youngster on a motorcycle, he has to release the youngster into the custody of his parents. And more than likely, his parents are the ones who have paid for the motorcycle and given the child permission to ride it.

England is also concerned that a youngster on a motorcycle will be seriously injured if a deputy chases him. An accident can happen during the chase, particularly if the youngster is trying to resist arrest.

Understandably, England doesn't want to get sued over a matter which is mostly a nuisance.

There is something people can do who are sick and tired of juvenile delinquents riding through their flower beds on their motorbikes. They can take out a warrant for the child's parents.

We hope this option will be exercised frequently when youngsters insist on disturbing the peace. The parents are, after all, responsible for their youngster's behavior. They should feel the full weight of the law.

---

1. This editorial is based on what issue?_____

2. What is the newspaper's opinion?_____

3. Are any facts used to support the paper's opinion? If so, what are these facts?_____

_____

4. Do you agree with the opinion? Explain why or why not._____

_____

Using the classified ads

Many newspaper readers would be lost without the classified ad section. This section tells them about job openings. It tells them where they can buy a doghouse or a used piano. It lists houses for sale. It also lists new and used cars for sale.

Have you ever used the classified section of your newspaper? Ads in this section are in alphabetical order. These listings are grouped under headings. These headings are called "classifications." There may also be classification numbers.

Activity 6

Reading the "classifieds"

Read the classified ads below. They are ads for apartments and used cars. Abbreviations are used in some of these ads. Answer the questions about these ads. Look for clues within the ads to help you figure out what the abbreviations stand for.

UNFURN. APTS.

4 LARGE RM APT — mod. kitchen & bath, h/hw suppl'd, 2 children accepted. call 926-0359

4 ROOM APT — H & HW Supl'd, Avail. Oct. 1st, So. 16th St. Area Sec. Req'd, Call 926-4658

4 ROOMS — H&HW supl'd, $295. Mo. + Sec. 1 child accepted Call 923-4772

4 ROOMS, H/HW, secure building. See Mark, Apt 8, 830 Clinton Ave. Immed. occup. 372-3919.

517 SO. 17th St. 4 rms & bath, HT/Hw incl. $235 + sec. Apply 2nd fl. front. or call 753-6471.

5 NICE RMS. 535 So. 19th St. Rent $165, supply own gas heat. Adults pref. Call eves 992-7199.

5 RMS. — 1st flr. 138 Huntington Terr. H/HW supplied. $310 + sec. Call 672-7266 between 6-10PM.

5½ RMS
$380/MO, H/HW
Call aft. 6, 374-2836

5 ROOM APT — near downtown. Heat & Hot Water sup'd. $265/Per mo + 1 mo security. Call 624-4399 or 356-4902.

5 ROOMS, 2 BR's, heat furnished, $270., sec required, adults only. Call aft 6pm 672-7786.

5 ROOMS - Adult cpl. preferred. Prefer no children, but will accept 1. 137 Seymour Ave.

Availabilities

COLONNADE APARTMENTS

Studio	$245★
1 Bedrooms	$300★
2 Bedrooms	$375★
2 BRS, Den + 2 Baths	$510★

★TYPICAL RENTS
SUBJECT TO AVAILABILITY
•24 HR GUARD SERVICE
• ON SITE PARKING
•BUSES TO N.Y.C.

Apartment Features
Included in Rent
•GAS
•HEAT & HOT WATER

Call   484-8300

1. How much is the rent for the apartment at 517 South 17th Street?

_____

2. Must the renter pay a security deposit for this apartment?_____

3. What number do you call to inquire about the 5½-room apartment that rents for $380 a month?_____

4. What four types of apartments can you rent at Colonnade?_____

_____

_____

_____

5. Which of the Colonnade Apartments is the least expensive?_____

_____

6. Which is the most expensive?_____

7. After reading these ads, what do you think these abbreviations mean?

rm._____

H/HW_____

sec._____

mod._____

avail._____

immed. occup._____

pref._____

cpl._____

CHECK YOUR UNDERSTANDING OF READING NEWSPAPERS

Here are some words you should know when you read and use a newspaper. Choose the correct word or words for the following sentences.

editorial	alphabetical	feature
index	obituary	classified ad

1. I can find the page in the newspaper that lists the movies for today by looking in the _____ .

2. A good way to find a used car is to look in the _____ section.

3. In today's _____ the editor argued against raising telephone rates.

4. Items in an index are usually listed in _____ order.

5. I saw the news of his death listed on the _____ page.

6. I enjoy _____ articles in the travel section.

Decide whether each of the following statements is TRUE (T) or FALSE (F).

_____ **7.** An editorial always tells all the facts about an issue.

_____ **8.** You can find a list of the restaurants in your neighborhood in the classified section of the newspaper.

_____ **9.** ''Letters to the editor'' in a newspaper are likely to contain the writers' opinions.

_____ **10.** Classified ads are grouped by subjects or classifications.

ANSWER KEY

READING LABELS

Activity 1, p. 3
Bufferin Label
1. Arthritis Strength Bufferin (analgesic tablets) **2.** minor aches and pains of arthritis and rheumatism **3.** two tablets **4.** every four hours; eight tablets in 24 hour period **5.** if pain persists for more than 10 days or redness is present **6.** (a) do not take without consulting a physician if under medical care; (b) keep this medicine out of children's reach; (c) in case of accidental overdose, contact a physician immediately

Vicks DayCare Label
1. Vicks DayCare (cold medicine) **2.** stuffy nose, congested sinus openings, coughing, headache pain, cough, irritated throat **3.** adults; one fluid ounce (2 tablespoonfuls); children: one-half fluid ounce (1 tablespoonful) **4.** every four hours; four doses per day (or 8 tablespoonfuls) **5.** persistent cough, high fever **6.** (a) do not use without consulting a physician if you have high blood pressure, diabetes, heart, or thyroid disease; (b) do not use more than 10 days unless directed by physician; (c) do not exceed recommended dosage unless directed by physician

Activity 2, p. 5
Sam's Drugs Label No. 2345
1. Geri Purshing **2.** Two **3.** Dr. Pillston **4.** four **5.** 0 (no)

Sam's Drugs Label No. 2346
1. Vicki Urkan **2.** One **3.** Dr. Jaons **4.** six **5.** 0 (no)

Check Your Understanding, p. 6
1. side effect **2.** symptom **3.** caution **4.** dose **5.** prescription

Activity 3, p. 7
Roxo Bleach Label
1. F **2.** F **3.** T **4.** T **5.** F

Flying Insect Killer Label
1. F **2.** F **3.** T **4.** F **5.** F **6.** F **7.** T **8.** T **9.** F **10.** T

Activity 4, p. 9
Ammonia Label
1. Rinse eyes thoroughly with water, preferably warm, for 15 minutes.
2. Give large quantities of diluted vinegar or juice of lemon, grapefruit, or orange. Call physician.
3. Flood with water, then wash with vinegar.
4. Flood with water, then wash with vinegar.

Red Demon Lye Label
1. Immediately hold face under running water for 20 minutes with eyes open, by force if necessary.
2. Clear mouth. Do not induce vomiting. Give [drink] large quantities of water or milk. Give at least 2 ounces to maximum of one pint equal parts of vinegar and water, followed by olive oil or cooking oil (by teaspoon). Transport victim to nearest medical facility or call physician immediately.
3. Flush with water for 15 minutes.
4. Flush with water for 15 minutes.

Check Your Understanding, p. 10
1. Spray surface generously. Wipe immediately with a clean, dry cloth.
2. container may burst
3. shake well
4. near fire or flame
5. container may burst
6. about six inches
7. no

Activity 5, p. 11
1. F **2.** T **3.** F **4.** T **5.** T

Activity 6, p. 12
1. B **2.** A,D,H **3.** C,D,H **4.** A **5.** A,D,E,G,H (note: label G is only label specifying "line-dry only") **6.** F,G **7.** A,E,G **8.** F

Check Your Understanding, p. 13
1. material treated to hold its shape and resist wrinkling (material that is 60% polyester and 40% cotton) **2.** wash with items similar in color **3.** no **4.** yes **5.** no

Activity 7, p. 15
Cost Cutter Corn Label
1. one cup **2.** two **3.** 210 **4.** A; C **5.** 6(%) **6.** calcium

Kroger Mixed Vegetables
1. one cup **2.** approximately one **3.** 70 **4.** 2,14 **5.** fat **6.** A; C **7.** 4(%) **8.** carrots, potatoes, celery, sweet peas, green beans, corn, lima beans, water, salt, ground onion **9.** 8½ oz. **10.** 8(%)

Activity 8, p. 17
1. 8
2. 80
3. 19g (grams)
4. aspartame (NutraSweet)
5. no
6. **Sugar Free Jello-O:** gelatin, adipic acid, maltodextrin, disodium phosphate, aspartame, fumaric acid, artificial color, salt, artificial flavor
   Regular Jell-O: sugar, gelatin, adipic acid, disodium phosphate, fumaric acid, artificial color, artificial flavor
7. General Foods Corporation, White Plains, NY 10625

Check Your Understanding, p. 19
1. 40 **2.** tomatoes **3.** two **4.** 2(%) **5.** A

FOLLOWING DIRECTIONS

Activity 1, p. 21
a. a **2.** c **3.** a **4.** c **5.** b

Activity 2, p. 22
See folded letters in Steps 3 and 4 (p. 23).

Activity 3, p. 23
1. F **2.** F **3.** T **4.** F **5.** T **6.** T **7.** T **8.** T **9.** F **10.** T

Activity 4, p. 25

IF YOU...	YOUR WATCH WILL DISPLAY...		
	TIME HRS: MINUTES	FLASHING SECONDS	MONTH & DATE
1. Press the TIME display button once.	✔		
2. Press the TIME display button and hold the button in depressed position.		✔	
3. Depress the TIME display button twice.			✔
4. Push the TIME display button twice and hold the button down after the second push.			✔

Setting the Month
1 Press the SET button once.
4 Release the TIME button when the number of the desired month appears.
3 Hold the TIME button down.
2 Look for a flashing month number indicating you are in the "month set mode."

Setting the Date
1 Press the SET button a second time.
4 Release the TIME button when the correct date appears.
3 Hold the TIME button down.
2 Look for a flashing date indicating you are in the "date set mode."

Setting Hours
1 Press the SET button a third time.
4 Release the TIME button when the correct hour is displayed.
3 Hold the TIME button down.
2 Look for a flashing date indicating you are in the "hours set mode."

Setting Minutes
1 Press the SET button a fourth time.
4 Release the TIME button when the correct minute appears.
3 Hold the TIME button down.
2 Look for a flashing minute indicating you are in the "minute set mode."

Check Your Understanding, p. 28
1. immerse 2. sequence 3. assemble 4. abrasive 5. peak performance 6. b 7. c 8. a 9. c 10. c

Activity 5, p. 30
1. c 2. e 3. a 4. d 5. f 6. b

Activity 6, p. 30
1. oz. 2. c. 3. gal. 4. lb. 5. tbsp. 6. qt. 7. tsp. or t. 8. dz. 9. sm. 10. pt. 11. pkg. 12. sq. 13. lg. 14. min.

Activity 7, p. 31
Pound Cake Recipe
1. One-half pound of (butter) 2. Five; one at a time 3. tube 4. one hour and 30 minutes; 350 degrees 5. fifteen 6. cold

Veg-A-Burger Recipe
1. 8-oz. can 2. cup 3. uncooked 4. drained 5. hamburger; onions 6. six

Activity 8, p. 33
Lemon Sponge Pie
1. no 2. yes 3. no 4. no 5. no 6. yes

Pizza
1. no 2. no 3. yes 4. yes 5. no 6. no

Check Your Understanding, p. 35
1. cup 2. teaspoon 3. quart 4. teaspoon 5. small 6. gallon 7. dozen 8. pound 9. tablespoon 10. pint 11. set oven temperature in advance 12. mash or beat until smooth 13. shred with a grater 14. heat to just below the boiling point 15. cook at low heat on top of stove

Activity 9, p. 38
Answers will vary.

Activity 10, p. 40
1. 4721 ✔ 4721
2. 584 ✔ 584
3. 80962 ___ 90862
4. 9325 ✔ 9325
5. 0365 ___ 0365
6. Louis Eldern ✔ Louis Eldern
7. James Meyer ___ James Mayer
8. Arthur Lungren ___ Arthur Lundgren
9. Frank Schaefer ✔ Frank Schaefer
10. Allan Kenmore ___ Albert Kenmore

Activity 11, p. 41
1. SAVE   part___   keep ✔   spend___   sort___
2. STAY   remain ✔   result___   leave___   press___
3. IDEA   story___   value___   thought ✔   subject___
4. GATHER collect ✔ choose___   remove___   decide___
5. HIRE   raise___   locate___   divide___   employ ✔
6. NEARLY every___   quickly___ almost ✔   never___

Activity 12, p. 45
1. A 2. C 3. A 4. A 5. D

Check Your Understanding, p. 46
1. applicant 2. tester 3. multiple-choice 4. horizontal 5. SAT 6. vertical 7. T 8. T 9. F 10. T

READING NEWSPAPERS

Activity 1, p. 48
Sports	Editorial	Classified Ads	Entertainment	Home Section
4,5	7	9	1,3,6,8	2,10

Activity 2, p. 49
Topics	Pages	Section
How to grow house plants	1–2	L
Tours to Las Vegas	1–6	J
What's in store for a Gemini today	19	C
Stamp collecting	5	J
Job openings	1–8(F) or 1–8(G)	F,G
Your favorite comic strip	2–8(L)	L
Stock averages	3–6	E

Activity 3, p. 50
Girls Don't Lag in Math
1. girls' ability to do math
2. A study was conducted by researchers from the University of Chicago.
3. to disprove, or contradict, the Johns Hopkins University study
4. Zalman Usiskin and two colleagues tested 1,366 high school students in geometry after both the boys and girls had been taught the material.
5. in classrooms across the country
6. 1,366
7. no
8. Scholastic Aptitude Tests (SAT)
9. Zalman Usiskin, Sharon Senk, and Roberta Dees
10. geometry

Pupils Go to Mat in Academic Olympics
1. a fourth grader at Dodge Elementary School, 2651 W. Washington Blvd.
2. became a champion in the District 9 Academic Olympics
3. West Side District (Crane High School auditorium, 2245 W. Jackson Blvd.)
4. They wanted to "elevate the achievements levels of their pupils."
5. the inner-city school districts

Activity 4, p. 53
1. Editorial 2. News Story 3. Editorial 4. News Story 5. Editorial 6. News Story 7. Editorial 8. News Story 9. News Story 10. Editorial

Activity 5, p. 54
1. disturbances by youngsters riding motorcycles
2. A child's parents should be held responsible for a child's actions while riding a motorcycle.
3. The sheriff has decided not to respond to calls complaining about youngsters riding motorcycles.
4. Answers will vary.

Activity 6, p. 55
Apartment Ads
1. $235 2. yes 3. 374-2836 4. studio, 1 bedroom, 2 bedrooms, 2 bedrooms with den and 2 baths 5. the studio 6. 2 bedrooms with den and 2 baths
7. rm.   room   avail.   available
   H/HW   heat/hot water immed. occup. immediate occupancy
   sec.   security   pref.   preferred
   mod.   modern   cpl.   couple

Check Your Understanding, p. 57
1. index 2. classified ad 3. editorial 4. alphabetical 5. obituary 6. feature 7. F 8. F (some urban newspapers might carry restaurant ads by neighborhood in their classified section) 9. T 10. T

NTC LANGUAGE ARTS BOOKS

Business Communication
Business Communication Today!
  Thomas & Fryar
Handbook for Business Writing,
  Baugh, Fryar & Thomas

Essential Skills
The Book of Forms for Everyday
  Living, *Rogers*
Building Real Life English Skills,
  Starkey & Penn
English Survival Series, *Maggs*
Essential Life Skills Series
Everyday Consumer English,
  Kleinman & Weissman

Genre Literature
Another Tomorrow: A Science Fiction
  Anthology, *Hollister*
The Detective Story, *Schwartz*
The Short Story & You, *Simmons &
  Stern*
You and Science Fiction, *Hollister*

Journalism
Getting Started in Journalism,
  Harkrider
Journalism Today! *Ferguson & Patten*

Language, Writing and Composition
An Anthology for Young Writers,
  Meredith
The Art of Composition, *Meredith*
Lively Writing, *Schrank*
Look, Think & Write, *Leavitt & Sohn*
Writing in Action, *Meredith*
Writing by Doing, *Sohn & Enger*

Media
Photography in Focus, *Jacobs &
  Kokrda*
Television Production Today! *Kirkham*
Understanding Mass Media, *Schrank*
Understanding the Film, *Johnson &
  Bone*

Mythology
Mythology and You, *Rosenberg &
  Baker*
Welcome to Ancient Greece, *Millard*
Welcome to Ancient Rome, *Millard*
World Mythology, *Rosenberg*

Reading
Reading by Doing, *Simmons & Palmer*

Speech
The Basics of Speech, *Galvin, Cooper
  & Gordon*
Contemporary Speech, *HopKins &
  Whitaker*
Creative Speaking, *Buys, et al.*
Creative Speaking Series
Dynamics of Speech, *Myers &
  Herndon*
Getting Started in Public Speaking,
  Prentice & Payne
Listening by Doing, *Galvin*
Literature Alive! *Gamble & Gamble*
Person to Person, *Galvin & Book*
Public Speaking Today! *Prentice &
  Payne*
Speaking by Doing, *Buys, Sills & Beck*

Theatre
The Book of Cuttings for Acting &
  Directing, *Cassady*
The Book of Scenes for Acting
  Practice, *Cassady*
The Dynamics of Acting, *Snyder &
  Drumsta*
An Introduction to Theatre and Drama,
  Cassady & Cassady
Play Production Today! *Beck, et al.*

For a current catalog and information about our complete line
of language arts books, write:
National Textbook Company,
a division of NTC Publishing Group
4255 West Touhy Avenue
Lincolnwood (Chicago), Illinois 60646-1975 U.S.A.